Without a Job, Who Am I?

Without a Job, Who Am I?

*Rebuilding Your Self When You've Lost
Your Job, Home, or Life Savings*

Abraham J. Twerski, M.D.

HAZELDEN®

Hazelden
Center City, Minnesota 55012
hazelden.org

Library of Congress Cataloging-in-Publication Data

Twerski, Abraham J.
    Without a job, who am I? : rebuilding your self when you've lost your job, home, or life savings / Abraham J. Twerski.
        p.   cm.
    Includes bibliographical references.
    ISBN 978-1-59285-832-3 (softcover)
    1. Life change events—Psychological aspects.   2. Self-esteem.   3. Adjustment (Psychology)   4. Unemployment—Psychological aspects.   5. Finance, Personal—Psychological aspects.   I. Title.
    BF637.L53T94 2009
    155.9'3—dc22

                                                            2009033653

Editor's note

The names, details, and circumstances may have been changed to protect the privacy of those mentioned in this publication.

This publication is not intended as a substitute for the advice of health care professionals.

Alcoholics Anonymous and AA are registered trademarks of Alcoholics Anonymous World Services, Inc.

Some stories in this book have been passed down through oral tradition, and the original sources are unknown to the author.

Some stories in this book have been quoted or retold from *The Sun Will Shine Again* with permission from the publisher, ArtScroll/Mesorah.

13 12 11 10 09   2 3 4 5 6

Interior design and typesetting by BookMobile Design and
    Publishing Services

To my loving wife, Gail,
*without whose inspiration and encouragement this
book would not have been possible*

Contents

Acknowledgments

I THANK the thousands of people who have shared their lives with me over the past fifty years.

Why I Wrote This Book

IT SEEMED TO COME OUT OF NOWHERE. True, a few economists had been issuing dire warnings for some time, but hardly anyone heeded them. Then, in the fall of 2008, the economic tidal wave struck, suddenly and furiously. Millions of jobs were lost, trillions of dollars of savings were wiped out, and mighty financial institutions crumbled. Homes were foreclosed and families were rendered destitute. People who had felt secure in their lives found themselves floundering without support. It was indeed an economic tsunami, and the backwash has devastated many of us.

A friend called me, suggesting I write something that might provide some moral support to victims of this disaster. Not wishing to be redundant, I visited a major bookstore to see what had already been published on the subject. I was surprised to find that although there were a number of books by economic pundits explaining the sources of the crisis and financial gurus with advice about money, there was nothing in the way of moral support for sufferers.

As a psychiatrist, I have been taught how to treat depression, and as a rabbi, I have tried to offer solace to people in grief. But neither of these skills appeared relevant to the mass upheaval resulting from the economic meltdown. Perhaps, I thought, the reason there are no books on the subject is that there is nothing one can say.

But that idea gave me no peace. When I entered medical school, I was told that the role of a physician is "to cure sometimes, but to relieve always." The heads of nations may confer on how to cure our economy's ills, but so far their efforts have not produced dramatic results. Some Band-Aid measures have been offered, but the wounds are too deep to be treated with mere Band-Aids. And even though the economy will no doubt turn around eventually, millions of people who have lost their jobs and savings will be feeling the effects of this crisis for some time to come.

Perhaps, I thought, I might find something in my fifty-plus years as a psychiatrist and a rabbi that might provide a modicum of comfort to the victims of the worst economic disaster in recent memory.

But what can one do for someone who is unemployed or is otherwise facing financial ruin? There is no way we can find a person a job when there are no jobs to be had. There's no way to restore the value of a 401(k) that is nearly worthless. The depression resulting from such devastating blows is not going to be relieved by Prozac, at least not for the long run.

As both a physician and cleric, I have felt the utter frustration of wanting to help someone who is suffering, but finding that I am powerless. What could I say to relieve some of their agony? I have been with parents who have lost a child and with patients who were told that there was no effective treatment for their cancer. But strangely, people do get some comfort, minuscule as it may be, from someone simply being *there* with them. There are few words of wisdom that can relieve the pain of these tragedies, and yet, by being completely silent, it may seem that we are indifferent, and that may make it worse.

Especially in the United States, people are motivated by and identify with the "American Dream" of success. The forms of such success are many, but they almost always include both financial comfort and career accomplishments. In fact, upon meeting a new person, we Americans are most likely to introduce ourselves in terms of *what we do for a living*. Usually, we assign a certain level of status and comfort to various occupations. This means we see ourselves, and other people, as having worth primarily in terms of the career we have (or once had, if we have now retired). But if a person is only what one does and what one earns, then what happens when that is taken away? One is left with nothing.

But there can be more, and indeed there *is* more to life, than what we do (or did) and what we earn.

As I pondered these questions, strangely enough, I was inspired by a comic strip in the newspaper—a cartoon that posed the question that is the title of this book and that suggested at least one answer. Beginning with that, I tried to find additional answers for people who ask or think the question, "Without a job, who am I?"

If reading this book brings any relief to these people, I will feel richly rewarded.

CHAPTER 1

Am I My Job?

For Better or For Worse © 1995 Lynn Johnston Prod. Reprinted by permission of Universal Press Syndicate.

PERHAPS YOU'RE FAMILIAR with the comic strip *For Better or For Worse* by artist Lynn Johnston, who has been documenting American middle-class life for three decades. In the strip above, the main character, Elly, has lost her job. She feels that her family may not be able to afford things they want, but husband John reassures her they can survive. Still, the furniture is not Elly's central problem. In exasperation, she cries out, "Without a job, who am I?" Daughter April knows better. Her mind has not been distorted by society's warped values. April embraces Elly, which says to her better than a thousand words could, "You're my mother, job or no job!"

Like Elly and John, we've been hit hard by the recent economic collapse. There's no minimizing the enormity of the problem of losing a job, having a home foreclosed, or seeing one's life's savings wiped out. But that should not destroy one's sense of self, one's feeling of worthiness. A job is a way of earning a livelihood, which is certainly of great importance. Nevertheless, no job or house, no stock portfolio or retirement fund should be our entire identity.

Unfortunately, this identification prevails in our culture. When we first introduce ourselves to someone, we're likely to begin with, "I am a lawyer," or "I am a plumber," or "I'm a salesman." People say what they *do* rather than who they *are*. We may refer to ourselves as human *beings,* but many of us really function as human *doings.* Consequently, if the *doing* is lost, one feels one is nothing.

Why?

Our culture has brainwashed us. Money and material things are indeed important, but they have taken on disproportionate significance.

Don't get me wrong. I know that losing one's job (or home or savings) is among the most devastating things that can happen to a person, but if you have true self-esteem, it shouldn't destroy you—and if it does, then you may have too much of your identity in your job or your money.

There are people who devote many hours to work so they can give their family things they want, but their involvement in work is so complete that they cannot give themselves to their family and to their friends and significant others. The fact is that if you believed more in your self-worth, you would realize that as important as it may be to provide your loved ones with material things, it is even more essential that you provide them with yourself.

You are a unique person with intelligence and sensitivity. *You* have the ability to love, to be considerate of and help others, to be happy and share in other people's joy, and to commiserate with them in their grief. *You* have the ability to choose between right and wrong, to act morally and ethically, sometimes in defiance of strong temptations. *You* have the ability to think about a purpose and goal in life, and you have the ability to work on making yourself a better person. *You* have the ability to control your anger, to forgive someone who offended or hurt you, and to apologize if you offended someone. These are the features that define you as a human being and distinguish you from other living creatures. These traits give you value as a human being, and these traits are not lost if you lose your job.

Too often, we tend to form an opinion of ourselves based on what others think of us and how they act toward us. These opinions and actions get tied up in how much we invest in our work roles. If a highly regarded college professor suffers a stroke and is unable to speak and teach and gather accolades as a teacher anymore, does that mean she isn't a worthwhile human being? It boils down to our belief in our intrinsic worth as people, untethered from our changing public roles and reputations.

Because we invest so much of our ego in what we do and what we can earn and what we own, we may feel that we have lost the respect of others when we are unable to earn and spend money. I heard of a person who had fallen on hard times and had prayed regularly at the same synagogue for twenty years who said, "I can no longer go there. I used to donate a hundred dollars regularly, but now I can barely afford to give ten." What a terrible mistake that someone could feel less worthy to the congregation where he worships because of changed material circumstances beyond his control.

So before we go any further in exploring this question— "Without a job, who am I?"—consider these simple actions you can take right away to show that you are indeed more than your work or your wealth.

Finding Your True Worth

First, nothing makes us feel better than helping somebody else who's in trouble. You probably know someone who has lost his job or retirement savings. Invite that person over for dinner or to spend an evening together. Show that you value the friendship. Not only will you be doing something nice for someone, you will be gaining something valuable, too: when you show respect and positive feelings for another person, you acquire them for yourself.

Next, if you have kids, make time to spend with them. Play a game, take interest in their homework and hobbies, and eat meals as a family. Let them know you care about them, and give them opportunities to show their concern and caring for you. No matter how big your problems may seem, sharing the load helps everybody. If you don't have kids, reach out to other family members and friends—not only to get help, but also to get outside yourself by showing an interest in others. You'll soon experience your value beyond what you earn and own.

In a 1996 study, researchers sought to identify why adolescents in some families had more problems than others. Hundreds of families were interviewed and tons of data analyzed. The result? The most significant factor wasn't how many things the family owned, or the parents' social standing or career success; it was simply that in the healthier families, *the family shared meals more often.* Another study by researchers at the University of Minnesota found that "the more frequently children ate with their parents the less likely they were to smoke, drink, use marijuana, or show signs of depression."[1] We can forget that a pleasant meal together can be a time to bond, to experience and share concern and support with the people we care about.

When times are tough, family members should draw closer to one another and show support, affection, and appreciation, like little April in the cartoon strip. If the stress of the economic crisis prompts family members to draw closer to one another, it may be a silver lining in this very dark cloud.

There's a simple exercise you can do that not only awakens gratitude for what you have but also helps you uncover some of the basic qualities that make you a unique person of value. When it seems that there's little to be grateful for, keeping a "gratitude journal" devoted specifically to paying attention to those things in our lives that we really can be thankful for can be a good antidote to one-sided negative thinking. While you're at it, you can record the daily incidents that demonstrate some of the positive qualities that make you unique as a human *being.* Your journal might contain simple entries such as these:

- I was looking for a parking space at the supermarket, and I saw someone getting ready to pull out. I waited and signaled, but another driver, who saw me waiting for that space, pulled in and grabbed it. I felt a surge of anger and was going to tell him off, but I decided it wasn't worth it.

- I was shoveling the snow off my sidewalk when I remembered that my neighbor had returned from the hospital a few days ago, so I shoveled his walk, too.
- Jane left the meat loaf in the oven too long and felt terrible about it. I kissed her and told her that her many delicious meat loaves more than made up for this one.
- The checkout clerk gave me an extra dollar in change, and I gave it back to her.
- I apologized to someone I had reamed out last week.
- I took the kids to visit my mother. She enjoyed them.
- I helped someone who was stranded at the side of the road with a flat tire.
- Jimmy was upset because he felt his teacher was unfair to him. I spent time listening to him, and he felt much better about it.

It's uplifting to pay attention to incidents like these. We remind ourselves that by acting on values such as compassion, honesty, and forgiveness, we realize our *real* worth—the worth that is deeper than that associated with job, career, or material success. We may also want to record some things that we could have done better, resolving how to handle a similar situation differently next time. Seeing how we improve our behavior and finding the motivation to do so is uplifting, too.

There's tremendous satisfaction in recognizing your uniqueness as a human being and finding the good in yourself that goes deeper than material success. Every person really is one-of-a-kind—there are no two sets of identical voice or fingerprints!—and you have the power to nurture and develop your unique identity.

When we don't pay enough attention to our uniqueness, when we have buried or forgotten our true identity, we may fabricate one that is hardly edifying. This point is illustrated by this tale about one of the "wise men" of Chelm, an old city in Poland that is the setting of many entertaining and instructive Jewish tales about our human foibles. Many of the villagers are remarkably stupid in a quaint sort of way, as the story shows.

One day, a citizen of Chelm was at the public bathhouse. It suddenly dawned upon him that without clothes, most people look alike. He became quite anxious with the thought, "When it comes time to go home, how will I know which one is me?" After pondering this a bit, he came up with a brilliant solution. He found a piece of red string and tied it around his great toe. He was now distinctly identifiable.

Unfortunately, as he sudsed and showered, the red string fell off his toe, and when another bather stepped on it, it stuck to his foot. When it was time to leave, the first bather looked at his foot, and seeing nothing on it, he was perplexed. Then he noticed the other man with the red string on his foot. He approached him and said, "I know who you are, but can you tell me, who am I?"

Some people seek an identity by having the equivalent of a red string. Their identity is the successful sales manager, the busy entrepreneur, the super-accomplished career woman and homemaker. Or it's the luxury automobile in the driveway or the impressive façade on the mansion. But this is hardly the lasting identity that comes from within. What happens if one sells the car or, worse, it is repossessed? Does one's identity go along with it?

A person can use a time of trouble to recover a genuine identity, one rooted in esteem not for what one does or has, but for what one *is*.

CHAPTER 2

Reacting to Crisis

EVEN IN TIMES OF WIDESPREAD LAYOFFS, reactions to economic adversity can vary across a wide spectrum, from mild to extreme. The variability can be due to many factors. First, situations differ—the stakes of a job loss may vary depending on one's age, family, finances, location, career path, and so on. Second, the type of support a person has varies; some people are deeply networked while others are all alone. And third, the types of experiences, fears, and expectations one brings to a loss vary dramatically as well.

Put simply, every person is different. Each of us reacts to the reality we perceive, but we must understand that "reality" is not objective. Two people may be exposed to the same situation but perceive it very differently. Consider two people with the same amount of savings, the same career, and the same family supports around them. Both lose their jobs on the same day. One person experiences the loss as a crisis; he feels anxious, afraid, helpless. Frozen, he stares out his window as bills accumulate. The other feels the loss but sees it as an exciting new challenge. She eagerly sets to work rearranging her life around the new circumstances. Given the same circumstances, two hundred people will have two hundred very different responses.

We are generally aware of what we feel and what we think, but what we are aware of is the contents of our *conscious* mind. We also have a *subconscious* mind, which is without question many times the size of the conscious mind. We may think of the subconscious mind as the hard drive of a computer on which *everything* we experience is automatically saved and nothing is ever deleted. We are familiar with the term *subconscious,* but to understand it better, it helps to know how the concept originated.

In 1889, Sigmund Freud, now known as the father of psychiatry, was attending a demonstration of hypnosis by Ambroise Liebeault in Nancy, France. Liebeault hypnotized a subject from the audience and gave him a classic "posthypnotic suggestion": after he awakened and returned to his seat, at a given signal, he would stand up and open his umbrella. He would have no memory that this suggestion had been given to him while under hypnosis.

After emerging from the hypnotic trance, the man returned to his seat, and Liebeault continued with his lecture. A few moments later, he made the gesture that was to serve as the signal. The man promptly arose and opened his umbrella. Liebeault asked him why he had done something so absurd as to open his umbrella indoors, and the man said that he could not explain his action. He just had an urge to do it, even though it made no sense to him. "Did anyone instruct you to do it?" Liebeault asked. "No," the man answered.

The audience was probably amused by this demonstration, but Freud was much more than amused. He realized that there *was* in fact a reason why the man opened his umbrella indoors. He had been instructed to do so. But if he could not remember the instruction, how could it motivate his action? It must be that ideas of which a person is totally unaware, or which are in the part of his mind that is *subconscious,* can affect a person's behavior. From there on, it was only a matter of elaborating this concept.[1]

The conscious mind operates according to the rules of logic. To the conscious mind, for example, incidents occurring in 1942 and 1992 are fifty years apart and cannot coexist. But to the subconscious mind, incidents separated by decades can be simultaneous. To the conscious mind, a creature such as a centaur (half man and half beast) is a nonexistent fantasy. But to the subconscious, there can be an individual who is comprised of two or more persons. The conscious mind can affirm or negate. The subconscious has no way of negating. (Think of dreams: dreams are the products of the subconscious mind, and a dream cannot show that something is not.) The conscious mind matures, so that the adult mind is much different from the juvenile mind. The subconscious mind does not mature.

A simple example of the nature of the subconscious mind is a phobia. A mature adult, strong and intelligent, sees a little puppy heading his way through his front yard. He panics and runs into the house. He has a dread of dogs, although he will readily admit that he knows a tiny puppy is harmless.

Why? At the age of three, this person was frightened when a huge dog jumped on him and barked. The subconscious recorded this incident and forever sees dogs as a dangerous threat. Forty years later, this person panics at the sight of a tiny puppy. Consciously, he knows it poses no danger, but to the subconscious, which never matured, the puppy is a ferocious dog. When the conscious and subconscious minds conflict, the subconscious usually wins.

When Alvin was a child, his father abandoned the family. His mother was unable to provide for the family, she lost the home, and the children were farmed out to relatives. Alvin's stay with an uncle was unpleasant. To the uncle, Alvin was an unwelcome burden, and he eventually sent the boy off to another relative. Alvin felt much shame, sensing that he was unwanted, and his being shuffled between relatives left him with deep feelings of insecurity.

Alvin managed to fend for himself and eventually became an accountant. When the economic crisis hit in 2008, he was laid off. Although there was no serious danger of losing his home, the widespread foreclosures resurrected Alvin's memory of being homeless and cast among unwilling relatives. Alvin's perception of reality was appreciably altered by the abandonment and homelessness of his childhood. Those experiences remained in his subconscious and were as fresh as if they had occurred yesterday, and he was in dread of losing his home.

Reassurance, even if realistic, may not be effective because reassurance speaks to the *conscious* mind, whereas anxiety originates in the subconscious mind. But there are therapeutic techniques that can reach the subconscious mind and reduce or eliminate anxiety. Hypnotherapy, by relaxing the conscious mind, may allow such access.

Everything we experience is processed through the subconscious mind. If you pass a sheet of white paper under a blue light it will appear to be blue. In much the same way, current experiences that pass through the subconscious mind are "colored" by whatever is there, and that is how we perceive them.

The usual occurrences in everyday life, even if colored by the subconscious mind, generally do not cause any problems, except in cases such as a phobia. But when something of greater significance happens to us, we may perceive it not as what it is in reality, but rather as how our subconscious sees it, and we may react accordingly.

And so, our subconscious mind, which has been accumulating and interpreting experience our entire lives, shapes the responses we have to today's events. This is why two hundred people in exactly the same circumstances today will have two hundred different responses. And this is why some will derive energy and joy from their new circumstances, while others will be frozen and sad.

Shame—and Its Antidote

Some people who have been laid off have profound feelings of shame. To feel depressed at the loss of one's job is understandable, but why shame?

One reason is that our minds have long memories, just as our bodies do. Think of immunizations. When we get a shot to immunize us against tetanus as children, the body produces a huge amount of antibodies in response. These antibodies gradually disappear from the bloodstream, so that by age twenty, hardly a trace of tetanus antibody can be detected. Then a person receives a "booster" shot, and immediately the body reacts by producing a huge amount of antibody, just as it had done years earlier. The body "remembers" and reproduces the initial response.

Shame is a very common reaction to losing one's job, one's

home, or one's savings. Unfortunately, shame is not very helpful as a response to the economic crisis. One might just as well feel ashamed for catching the flu during a flu epidemic. But at least, if one catches the flu, one will find a doctor. Someone who loses a job to the recession and feels shame may be frozen in place, incapable of seeking help. Let's see why shame freezes us and where it comes from.

First, let's distinguish between *shame* and *guilt*. One feels *guilt* if one senses having done something wrong. The good news is that one can make amends for a wrong deed, and there are ways of correcting one's behavior to eliminate the guilt. *Shame*, on the other hand, is the feeling that one is inherently bad. A child may be humiliated or made to feel bad, even though he cannot understand why. To put it another way, guilt is "I made a mistake," whereas shame is "I *am* a mistake." Because shame may not be related to a specific act, it is much more difficult to overcome. John Bradshaw elaborates on this in his book *Healing the Shame That Binds You.*[2]

Logically, there is no reason to feel either guilt *or* shame when one is laid off. However, as we have seen, shame is an all-too-common reaction. This irrational feeling might be easy to overcome were it not that it acts like a booster shot and recalls the distressing feelings of shame that one experienced in childhood. Just as the body reacts with a huge output of antibodies, the mind, too, remembers and may react with a great deal of shame.

So, although we should not, logically, be feeling shame, we may indeed feel that way, and it is as real to us as feeling a burn when we touch a hot stove. Feelings are not imaginary. The reason for our feelings may not be valid, but the feelings themselves are very real.

It is difficult to doubt the veracity of a sense experience. A person may have auditory, visual, or tactile hallucinations, and even the soundest arguments to the contrary are not likely to debunk a hallucination. A paranoid person who hears voices will not admit that the voices are imaginary, and a delusional person who sees insects all over him cannot understand why others do not perceive the reality that he sees.

Our psychological distortions of reality are just like sensory perceptions, and thus they generally resist logical argument. Unless these distortions are removed, a person's perception of reality will continue to be erroneous.

When a person is laid off, or his life's savings go up in smoke, his perception of the world may be distorted by these losses. He may be looking at the world through dark glasses, which causes him to see everything as dark—present, past, and future. In the darkness, he may overlook opportunities. Telling him that things will eventually change for the better will likely have no impact on him, nor will telling him that there is no reason for feeling shame. *Something other than logic is necessary to correct his misperception.*

The most effective method is that demonstrated by the child in the cartoon who embraces her mother and says, "Mum!" A warm hug says, "You mean much to me." *The expression of love can give a person a new lease on life.*

Love should be expressed between husband and wife, parents and children, friend and friend. Children should be taught that when daddy or mommy feels down, that's a time to show their parent extra love. People within the family tend to take things for granted: "Of course she knows I love her." It's always nice to be reminded, and love is especially effective as an antidepressant.

What is love? Author Liz Carpenter said it best:

Love is a moment and a lifetime. It is looking at him across a room and feeling that if I don't spend the rest of my life with him, I'll have missed the boat. Love is working together, laughing together, growing together. It is respect for each other and the people each cares about, however difficult it is sometimes to like his kinfolk or his friends. Love is wanting to shout from the rooftops the successes, little and big, of one another. Love is wanting to wipe away the tears when failure comes. Love is liking the feel of each other. It is wanting to have children together because they are the exclamation point of love. Love is laughter, especially in the middle of a quarrel.[3]

This is the love that can lift the screen of darkness from one's eyes and the heaviness from one's heart. It is not the self-gratifying drive that is no more love than fool's gold is gold, as the following story reveals.

A wise man observed a young man enjoying a dish of fish. "Why are you eating the fish?" the wise man asked. "Because I love fish," the young man answered.

"So," the wise man said, "it is because you love the fish that you took it out of the water, killed it, and cooked it. You do not love fish at all, young man. It is yourself that you love, and because you enjoy the taste of the fish, you killed it."

Unfortunately, much of what Western culture calls "love" is nothing more than "fish love," an exploitation that, rather than making another person feel good, may cause him or her to feel used. True love, as described by Liz Carpenter, gives a person a feeling of worthiness and can generate optimism and hope.

Many people, undone by the economic crisis, see the world as a dark place. Simple logical argument may not change their perception. True love can do it. True love means genuinely caring for the other person, respecting him and valuing him, and being ready to do anything that would help him feel better. True love is powerful and may be the only thing that can counteract the illogical negative feelings of shame and failure.

CHAPTER 3

Self-Esteem

I BELIEVE THAT SELF-ESTEEM is a significant determinant of human behavior. Furthermore, it appears to me that many, many people have a self-esteem problem to some degree.

Every person has a self-image and thinks of himself in a certain way. And, since a person is convinced that his self-image is valid, this is, therefore, his reality. For example, if a woman thinks she is unattractive for whatever reason, she will believe that everyone sees her as unattractive. I have seen very handsome people who thought of themselves as homely and very bright people who thought of themselves as dull. In relating to another person, whether it be an employer, a friend, or a social acquaintance, one relates according to what one believes the other person will see.

I am bold enough to say that *every* human being has a self-esteem deficit of some kind. The person who acts as though he is God's gift to the world may actually have very low self-esteem: presenting an attitude of superiority to the world may actually be a defense against the distress of low self-esteem. Ironically, people who are gifted are apt to have lower self-esteem than others who are less endowed.

Some people know that they are indeed excellent in some ways, but may feel markedly inferior in other ways. I know a physician with a large practice who used to come to the hospital at six a.m. on workdays. After seeing all his patients, he would interpret electrocardiograms, participate in a variety of meetings, teach medical students, and lecture to student nurses. He would then go to his private office, return to the hospital at six p.m., and keep himself busy with hospital work until nearly midnight. The nurses assumed that he avoided home because his wife was an impossible person to live with.

This doctor's wife consulted me and said, "You know how devoted John is to his practice and to the hospital. I am a very needy person, and I've often needed a shoulder to rest my head on, but he was never there for me. Our children grew up without a father. He treated them when they were sick, but otherwise he did not relate to them."

I happened to know this physician well. He was a wonderful human being who could have been emotionally supportive to his wife and children, but he was not aware that he had anything to offer them *as a person*. Feeling he had nothing to offer as a husband and father, he was uncomfortable at home. The only place he felt competent and worthy was in the hospital. This is not an uncommon phenomenon.

How Low Self-Esteem Interferes with Accepting Help

Why are feelings of inferiority so common? One reason might be that children feel minuscule in a world that is designed for adults.

Many years ago, a group of psychologists constructed an experimental house whose dimensions were proportioned for adults as a normal house is for children. The ceilings were thirty feet high, the seats of the chairs four feet high, the doorknobs seven feet high, and so on. In the study, some perfectly healthy, normal adults lived in this house for some time, and by the third day they were manifesting neurotic symptoms! But this is the kind of world our children live in—and it's the kind of world we grew up in. The feeling of being minuscule and helpless may arise in this fashion, and may not be completely eliminated as one matures. We may carry these feelings of inadequacy in our subconscious long after we have mastered the world around us. If, during childhood, our parents were neglectful and abusive, this greatly increases our feelings of inferiority. And no doubt even the best of parents inadvertently caused us to feel inferior at times: comments such as "You are so clumsy" or "You are stupid," said by an ordinarily loving parent in a moment of frustration, can seriously depress a child's self-esteem. A parent may not have any bad intentions when saying "Why can't you be like your sister?" but such a remark may scar a child.

How might feelings of inferiority affect us if we lose a job or lose our home? In today's economic crisis, people need help. Yet people with low self-esteem may *resist* offers of help. The reason is simple: they see their need for help as an indication that they are inadequate.

Let's see how such low self-esteem plays out in real life. I know of an excellent physician, a man who always presented himself as in control and proved himself to be a master at every job he took on. One day, he suffered a heart attack and was confined to the intensive care unit while in early recovery. On his third day in the intensive care unit, he ripped off the monitors, removed the intravenous drip, and stormed (albeit shakily) out of the hospital. Though he did not die, his foolish actions caused his recovery to take much longer than it should have. Why did he do this? After all, as a doctor, he knew full well the importance of careful attention and rest in his condition. In fact, he had prescribed just such care for countless patients, and he'd even scolded them for failing to follow his instructions.

The answer lies in his nucleus of low self-esteem. His bravado, his control, his need to show himself as the master of every task: these were actually ways of masking, from himself and from others, his deep, permanent sense of vulnerability and inferiority. These fearful feelings *required* that he present himself as independent and powerful by treating patients. When the tables were turned—when he became the patient, dependent and needy of help from nurses—he could not tolerate the blow to his self-esteem. It was anathema to him. Better to risk death than to show that he needed help.

With healthy self-esteem, one should be able to accept help when it is called for. And even without healthy self-esteem, one *will* need to learn to accept help when it is offered.

Bravado and the refusal of help are one manifestation of low self-esteem. Another is the constant sense of guilt or responsibility for events that one has no control over. Some people with low self-esteem are inordinately self-critical or apt to apologize—to assume responsibility—for everything that happens near them, regardless of their role in it. When such a person loses her job or sees her investments crash along with the stock market, her tendency to be self-critical results in her feeling responsible for the loss anyway. For example, one of my patients cried as she described her distress to me one day, then said, "I'm sorry for crying to you."

"It is perfectly normal to cry when one feels pain," I said. "There is no need to apologize for it."

The patient said, "I always apologize for everything."

"Stop doing that. Apologize only when you've actually done something wrong."

"Okay," she said. As she left the office, she saw someone in the waiting room. I overheard her saying, "I'm sorry I took so much of the doctor's time."

As you can see, behavior patterns are stubborn. Those that come with low self-esteem—whether manifested as bravado and the refusal to accept help, or as weak self-confidence—can interfere with the way one faces the challenges that come with loss of job, career, and material comfort. These feelings can make one refuse help or feel that one's condition is hopeless. In either case, change will be difficult.

Low Self-Esteem and Response to Challenges

When confronted with a challenge, there are only two possible reactions: *cope* or *escape*. Though it may seem like a third option, *ignoring* a problem is also a form of escape. (Think of a laid-off person who refuses to open bills or pay the rent or the mortgage, as if ignoring the problem would make it go away!)

How do we decide how to react? We size up the magnitude of the challenge and assess our ability to cope. If you are stalled on the railroad tracks and hear an oncoming locomotive, the only reasonable thing to do is leave the car, because the challenge of pushing it off the tracks is far beyond your capacity. But if you are the train's engineer and see a car stalled on the tracks, it is reasonable to jump into action and stop (or at least slow) the train.

These solutions to impending crisis seem obvious and simple. Yet in real life, self-esteem issues block our responses. A challenge may well be realistically within one's coping ability, but if one has low self-esteem, one may not *feel* capable of coping with it, and one may use any one of many escapist maneuvers. Perhaps the stalled driver felt he lacked the skill and strength to leave the car—and so he froze in place, in essence escaping the decision. Or ponder the events if the engineer felt incapable of braking the train. She escapes the decision to act and lets the train hit the car at full speed. The lesson is clear: *Escaping from a challenge that is within one's coping abilities is always self-destructive.*

People who *are* capable of adapting to the economic crisis but do not *feel* capable may miss opportunities. Even though they have accomplished much in the past, deep down they may see themselves as habitual losers. The feeling of inadequacy and the vision of being a habitual loser combine to rob them of motivation. They freeze in place, just like the driver on the train tracks. Rather than coping with the issue at hand—dealing with the financial and emotional impact of economic loss, they escape the decision. They freeze in place rather than taking action.

You may find yourself in this position. Take heart; it's a normal response, even if it is not the most productive one. Your work will involve learning to take action—and as you act, you will feel better.

Low Self-Esteem and Relationships

Low self-esteem can be destructive to many relationships, and this is even more apparent in the current economic crisis. A woman consulted me, saying, "I don't know what's come over my husband. We've had a wonderful marriage, and we have three lovely children. In the past few months he has turned into some kind of tyrant. I just can't take it."

What had happened? A few years earlier, when their youngest child began attending a full day of school, the woman had returned to school to train as a social worker. Her husband was in home construction, and he was very supportive of her course. She was fortunate to find work well before the recession. Once the recession started, her husband's formerly lucrative business slowed dramatically. Though he was still working some, his income and hours were greatly reduced. Rather than expressing gratitude that with his wife's additional income they could keep their home, he did a 180-degree turnaround, criticizing everything she did and even habitually causing her to be late for her job. The pattern had begun even before his own work and income were reduced, but had worsened now. "I don't know what's gotten into him," she said.

I met with the husband, and it was evident that he suffered from very low self-esteem. He did not feel that he deserved to be loved and was, therefore, very insecure about whether his wife truly loved him. He felt threatened that one day she might leave him. As long as she was dependent on him for support, this fear was suppressed. But when she began earning money for the household and he lost his own primary breadwinner role, he felt that if she were financially independent, her reason for staying with him would be weakened. He therefore tried to restrict her earning capacity. Once he understood this pattern, he entered into group therapy geared toward self-esteem enhancement, and their relationship flourished.

It is tragic to go through life thinking less of oneself than one deserves—to discount one's strengths and history. And it is particularly important to elevate one's self-esteem in adapting to the current crisis.

Having a job and being financially secure greatly enhance one's self-image, and when these are jeopardized, one's self-esteem may plummet. When this occurs, a person's mindset may take on a negative character: one looks at the world through dark glasses. Not only does the future seem bleak, but one may also look back at the past and fail to see anything good there either. This is why paying attention to self-esteem is so important when one has been hit hard by the economic recession.

The Components of Self-Esteem

How can we maximize self-esteem? First, it is important to understand its three principal components: *belongingness, worthiness,* and *competence.*

Belongingness

In order to have self-esteem, a person must feel significant—that is, wanted and needed by someone. This is what I mean by *belongingness.* Consider the opposite of belongingness: a sense of insignificance and isolation. It is devastating to feel that one is superfluous.

There are many ways in which one can feel belongingness. Certainly one belongs to one's family. A person may also feel a sense of belonging in a workplace, a congregation, a school, a political party, various other organizations, or the community. Youngsters who feel alienated may join a gang to feel that they belong somewhere. Some people may find belongingness in a pet. They feel wanted when their dog welcomes them home, for example. The loss of a pet may elicit grief equal to that of the loss of a beloved person.

Historically, one of the most powerful tools to bring people into social compliance is *excommunication*. Whether this tool is wielded by religion or by society, it strikes at the very core of belongingness. Although being laid off is not punitive, it nevertheless deprives a person of a source of belongingness. It can feel a bit like excommunication.

Inasmuch as we "need to be needed," we may search for belongingness by *making ourselves needed by others*. It is not uncommon for parents to make their children totally dependent on them. Their behavior may appear to be rooted in concern for the child, but they may be motivated by their own need to belong. Parents' urge to find belongingness by keeping their children dependent is the reason for the "empty nest syndrome": when children leave home, parents feel they are no longer needed.

We naturally have a sense of belongingness at work. Obviously, we are employed because we are needed in the workplace. When we are laid off, this source of being needed is lost, and we may seek to compensate by reinforcing other sources of belongingness: for example, we may unwittingly increase pressure on family members.

Worthiness

Belongingness is often intertwined with a sense of *worthiness*. Are we worthy of other people's attention, admiration, or validation? Are we using our life in ways that are worthwhile? A person who feels worthy has greater reason to feel desired by others. The reciprocal is also true: the feeling that one *belongs* adds to one's sense of worthiness.

Generally, people feel worthy because of what they do, especially when contributing in any way to others. If our contributions are acknowledged and appreciated by others, this reinforces the feeling of worthiness.

Unfortunately, sometimes our contributions go unnoticed. This may lead to resentments. We think, "I've done so much for them, and I am not appreciated." It is important, therefore, to be aware of the good one has done, even if others have not shown adequate appreciation. It helps to give oneself positive strokes by making a list. For example:

- I do a good job for my employer.
- I help others when they need it.
- I give of my time and effort to my family.
- I am a good listener to my friends.
- I stand up in situations that are unfair.
- I am loyal to my friends.

Competence

The third ingredient is *competence*. Competence is the sense of mastery—that we have the skills (or know how to develop the skills) to get the things we need in life. For many of us, what we do at work is an expression of our competence. In fact, we may have been complimented (or may have complimented others) for competence at work. The loss of a job therefore can feel like a deprivation of the very thing that makes us feel competent. The conditions of our loss can worsen that sense. For example, if the workforce was reduced and we were one of those let go, it's hard not to perceive that as a statement about our competence—despite the many other possible reasons that we were one of those chosen for the cut.

Let's assume for a moment, though, that our competence at work *was* one of the reasons why we were chosen for the cut. Maybe not the whole reason, but a part of it. That is truly a blow—*if* we have attached all of our sense of competence to our work performance. This, of course, means we are not attending to our other great competencies—as a friend, as a gardener, as a decent human being who makes the world just a little better place—whatever those qualities may be.

The blow to our sense of competence makes us feel bad, and we tend to forget all our other skills and gifts. When we're in a negative mode, we tend to focus on our mistakes and kick ourselves for what we've done wrong. No one goes through life without making mistakes, not even the most competent people. It is important to know how to handle mistakes so that they don't bring us down.

Why do we make mistakes? Because we did not recognize a decision or an act as a mistake when we made it. Our ability to foresee the future is limited, and we cannot always predict the consequences of a particular act.

But sometimes we repeat a mistake, when we should have learned from previous experience. This may happen because we just forgot how things turned out last time. Sometimes it is because we think there is no alternative. Sometimes we don't think because we act as a matter of habit. Sometimes we are so overwhelmed by a drive that we just deny the consequences: think of alcoholics who deny that their drinking has anything to do with their mistakes. In these cases, only a "rock-bottom" incident may break through the denial.

If we learn from mistakes, we convert a negative incident into a positive one. I was once told that one of the tires on my car needed to be replaced, but I did not want to spend the money. The tire went flat on a deserted country road, and it was four hours before I could get help. I learned to pay better attention to warnings. Such mistakes may be costly, but they are valuable learning experiences.

If we have low self-esteem, we may make the greatest mistake of all, which is to deny that we made a mistake. We may become defensive and try to justify our behavior. This is inevitably futile and only compounds the mistake. *Admitting a mistake* need not threaten our feeling of competence. To the contrary, admitting a mistake and learning from it should increase our sense of competence. At the same time, owning up to the truth boosts our feelings of worthiness. In addition, people are much more likely to associate with someone who admits a mistake than someone who believes he is always right. In this way, worthiness, belongingness, and competence all come together.

Getting Comfortable with Who I Am

As difficult as our economic conditions are right now, there are occasionally some opportunities, even if they may not be the greatest. And as the economy recovers, there will be more—but we must be in shape to take advantage of them. If we are down on ourselves and have a negative attitude, we may miss an opportunity, or even sabotage an opportunity. The following story is a classic example.

> *A young man's efforts to have a romantic relationship were failing dismally. He never had a second date. He finally gave up, assuming that no woman would be attracted to him. In his heart, he felt that if a woman saw who he really was, she would not be interested in him. Therefore, when dating, he tried to act in a*

way that he thought would show him in a better light. Because this was a put-on, it failed every time.

One day a friend whose cousin Lois was in town got tied up at the last minute and asked the young man to do him a favor and take Lois out to see the city.

So the young man took Lois out as a favor. He was not interested in being attractive to her. He was just doing his buddy a favor. Since he was not trying to impress her, he was relaxed and did not put up a front. As you may have guessed, she fell in love with him, and eventually they married.

If we are not comfortable with our real selves, we may try to act in a way that we think will make us more desirable. This may backfire, because the artificiality will come through to others. That's why self-esteem is so important in everything we do.

Tony was job hunting as an accountant. He heard that the head of the firm was an avid fisherman. Tony felt that if he could engage the boss in talking about fishing, this would impress him. The problem was that Tony knew nothing about it. So he spent the next two days cramming knowledge about fishing.

When he entered the boss's office, sure enough, he saw a picture on the wall of the boss holding up a large fish that he had caught. After talking about his qualifications for the job, Tony commented on the picture ana complimented the boss on his catch. Had he stopped there, his presentation would have been good. But Tony seized the opportunity to ask the boss where he had caught the fish and what he had used for bait, and proceeded to demonstrate his newly acquired knowledge about fishing.

He shot himself in the foot. The boss could see that Tony had never held a fishing rod in his hands. Despite Tony's excellent qualifications, the boss never called him for a second interview. It wasn't his lack of fishing skills that bothered the boss. It was Tony's "fishy" story. The boss needed someone who was honest, comfortable in his own skin, not someone who would pretend to be something he was not.

Make a personal inventory. Write down the things you are good at and the things that you're *not* good at. Those limitations that are real will not stand in your way. No person can be good at everything. It's when we are good at something but don't recognize it that we cause ourselves unnecessary hardships.

Here's how I learned to do what I was good at, which is one of the basic ingredients in self-esteem. My story is not unlike that of Tony, who pretended he could fish in an attempt to get a job. In this case, I also tried to "buy" a skill where I had none. But the mistake helped me find my true calling and my true sense of self.

As a youngster I was a rabid baseball fan. Those were the days of the true baseball greats—Babe Ruth, Lou Gehrig, Ted Williams—and I would've loved to play baseball, but I couldn't hit a ball nor catch a ball to save my life. Of course, the kids never wanted me on their teams, but I was desperate to play.

A block away from the playground was a sporting goods store that displayed a handsome, shiny Louisville Slugger bat. The kids would press their noses against the window to marvel at the bat, whose price, at $1.25, was astronomical. (In 1938, a family of four lived comfortably on thirty dollars a week.) To us, it seemed that only a millionaire could afford to pay $1.25 for a bat. But that bat was my only hope to get on a team.

I actually had $1.25 in my piggy bank, and I bought the bat. The kids' eyes popped out when I brought the coveted bat to the playground. "Lookit! The kid got the bat. Hey, kid, can we use the bat?"

"Only if I play," I said.

The two team captains chose sides, and I was left unchosen. One captain said, "What are we going to do with him? It's his bat." The other captain said, "Why don't you take him?" "Why should we take him?" the first captain said. "We've already got Eddie, and he stinks." The negotiations about which team would get stuck with me continued until one captain, with Solomonic wisdom, said, "Okay, we'll take him, but his outs won't count."

When it was my turn to bat, I waved at the ball and struck out. I eventually got tired of this charade and let the kids use the bat without my participation.

Being unsuccessful in sports, I devoted myself to academics, where I succeeded. Here's the key: my ineptitude as an athlete did not undermine my self-esteem, because this was a limitation *in reality;* it wasn't imaginary. *Low self-esteem occurs when one is unaware of the strengths one actually possesses.*

Making a list of your personality assets and limitations can help you gain a more accurate self-image. Of course, you may write down limitations that are imaginary rather than real. The solution to that problem is to review your inventory with a close friend and get an objective opinion of your self-perception.

I picked up this list-making technique in my treatment of alcoholics, whose recovery program requires that they make a "fearless moral inventory," then share it with another person. This worked for me, and it will work for you.

Fear of Failure

Who am I? So far we've focused on this question in the context of the current economic crisis, a situation filled with factors beyond our control, one in which our sense of utter powerlessness can compound the depression we may feel. But any number of occurrences can cause a person to wonder, "Who am I?" Those of us who suffer from unwarranted low self-esteem are most vulnerable to feeling crushed by any kind of adversity or reversal—including the current economic circumstances—that is beyond our personal control. We tend to "personalize" such circumstances as though they are our fault. They are not; this is a false conclusion.

To show how low self-esteem can lead us to this false conclusion, I'd like to share a personal experience, one that has left a scar that has not completely healed after nearly fifty years.

This happened in the first several months of my psychiatric training. One of the hospitalized patients under my care was Cynthia, a depressed seventeen-year-old who had dropped out of high school. My supervisor told me that it was essential for her recovery that she return to school, and he suggested that I personally drive her to school every day.

I did as I was told. I said to Cynthia, "You are going to school tomorrow. I will be here at eight tomorrow morning, and I expect to see you waiting outside."

Sure enough, Cynthia was waiting at eight a.m. I drove her to school, and when she returned, I discussed her day at school with her. This continued for several days, and it indeed appeared to be lifting her depression.

One day, I was called to the director's office. "I hear that you have been driving Cynthia to school," he said. I said, "Yes, that's what Dr. R. advised me to do."

The director shook his head. "Dr. R. may do that, but you must understand that I cannot allow one of my residents to take a young woman in his car. I trust you, Abe, but I cannot make any exceptions."

I explained the situation to Cynthia. "I'm sorry I can't drive you, but when you return from school tomorrow, we'll go over the day's events."

The following morning—December 6—is a day I will recall to the end of my life. I was informed that as she walked to school, Cynthia jumped off a bridge and was killed.

For me, that felt like the end of my career. I felt personally responsible for the death of that young woman. When you are hit with a trauma like that, you may ask "Who am I?" Not too many failures in life pack a wallop like that.

All my colleagues came to offer me support, but it was of little help. I was crushed.

The director said to me, "I share in your feelings, because you were following my orders." He pointed out that any psychiatric treatment entails uncertainty and risk, and that these may vary with the setting. "There are state hospitals that have very few suicides. Their patients may stay there for years and decades. Cynthia was our thirty-third suicide, but our average stay is several weeks, and we get people to go on with their lives. If you are going to try to be a risk-free psychiatrist, you may be able to do so, but not too many of your patients will improve."

Sensing my feelings of worthlessness, he continued, "You're going to be a damn good psychiatrist, Abe. Don't ruin it by trying to be perfect."

Of course, as you read this story, you may be seeing what others saw then: Abe did not make Cynthia jump from that bridge. He did not give the orders to drive her to school or to stop driving her to school—his supervising psychiatrist did. He was a novice in his career and was not even aware that there would be rules governing such a situation.

And you are correct. My mistake, if you wish, was in assuming Dr. R. knew the rules, and, once informed of the rules, in not foreseeing that Cynthia should not go to school unescorted. But that rational assessment doesn't reflect how I *felt* the event. Remember how a piece of white paper held under blue light will appear blue? I perceived Cynthia's suicide according to the "light" I shone on it—the dictates of my subconscious, with its own skewed logic. My urge to be perfect—to never make a mistake, to never fail—was tied to my hidden inner sense that *I was not worthy*. I had to defend myself against that sense of unworthiness by never failing. And that, as I have shown in our earlier discussion, was tied to my own low self-esteem.

Today, I am pleased with my career. And I have made progress with my self-esteem. Yet every December 6 I reexperience, even if only for a few moments, that feeling, "If I've failed, who am I?"

My experience with Cynthia is what I refer to as a "bottom-line" failure. I have come to realize that what I did was right, in spite of the tragic outcome.

Don't allow your self-esteem to depend totally on your successes. My director was right. The real failures are people who set their standards so low that they never run the risk of failure.

Now, when I revisit the story of Cynthia, I am able to see it in a new light. Who am I? I am a person with a deep sense of responsibility, and that gives me a feeling of worthiness.

The "Who am I?" question has many variations. Who am I as a parent if my children have severe problems? Who am I as a spouse if my marriage has failed? Who am I as a business-man if my firm has gone bankrupt? Who am I as a provider if I have lost my job and my savings?

The answer? Let me repeat: You are a unique person with intelligence and sensitivity. You have the ability to love, to be considerate of and help others, to be happy and share in other people's joy, and to commiserate with them in their grief. You have the ability to choose between right and wrong, and to act morally and ethically, sometimes in defiance of strong temptations. You have the ability to think about a purpose and goal in life, and you have the ability to work on making yourself a better person. You have the ability to control your anger. You have the ability to forgive someone who offended or hurt you, and to apologize if you have offended someone. These are the features that define you as a human being and distinguish you from other living creatures. These traits give you value as a human being, and these traits are not lost if you lose your job or experience a failure.

CHAPTER 4

Self-Fulfillment and Real Happiness

ONE REASON we come to tie our identities to our careers and bank accounts is that we have been influenced by "bottom-line thinking." This kind of thinking may give us an easy way to measure success, but it can prevent us from realizing our true worth.

Commerce rightfully operates according to the bottom line. If a person starts a business in a reckless manner, violating every logical consideration, and yet comes up with a windfall profit, many people in our society would say that the success validates his technique and they would consider him a shrewd businessman. To these "bottom-liners," his decision was a good decision. On the other hand, if someone starts a business with careful market analysis and consultation and yet, due to outside factors beyond her control, her business fails, to our bottom-liners, her venture shows bad decision making. To them, good and bad are "bottom-line" judgments.

This kind of thinking might carry some weight in the competitive business world, where the primary goal is to make a profit. But moral decisions need to be judged by higher standards if they are to indeed reflect the lasting values that make us human.

Now imagine this scenario. An unscrupulous, avaricious surgeon in desire of a fee convinces a patient of the need for exploratory surgery. He happens to discover and remove a small cancerous tumor that would have gone undetected for a long time and would have eventually been fatal. The unjustified surgery happens to save the patient's life, so bottom-line thinking would appear to have justified this surgeon's behavior. But if we look at this surgeon's behavior from an ethical perspective, wouldn't we still have to say he's a scoundrel?

Another surgeon has a patient who poses a difficult problem. Without surgery, he will die within months. Successful surgery can prolong his life for several years. However, he is a poor surgical risk: he very possibly may not survive the surgery—yet it is the only hope for prolonging his life. The surgeon agonizes over the case, consults with several specialists, and discusses the pros and cons with the family. The decision is reached to operate. In spite of all precautions and excellent surgical technique, the patient dies. The result was unfortunate, but we would still have to say that this surgeon is an ethical doctor.

If one applies bottom-line thinking, the unscrupulous surgeon's decision was good, and the honest, virtuous surgeon's decision was bad. But from a moral perspective, the latter surgeon was good even though the patient died, and the former surgeon was bad even though he saved the person's life.

It is not uncommon for devoted, caring parents to have a child who is antisocial, and for negligent, abusive parents to have a child who is an ideal, noble person. Yet, no matter what the bottom-line outcome is in these cases, the former are still good parents and the latter are still bad parents.

The Infantile Mind

The infantile mind is limited to what the child perceives as bottom-line values. Sweet is good; bitter is bad. A new toy is good; a pinprick, even one that will immunize him to dreaded diseases, is bad. To the juvenile, pleasure is a goal. As we mature physically, we should also mature emotionally and morally so that our values change. We may partake of the goods of the world en route to an ultimate goal of becoming the best person we can be. If our juvenile values do not change, the pursuit of pleasure as the prime goal in life can result in obesity, compulsive gambling, drug addiction, and yes, "money addiction."

When I was a child, my mother told me a bedtime story that I came to appreciate only many years later.

> A poor man made a wish that he would have a purse that would never be empty. The next morning, he found a magic purse that contained a dollar. When he removed the dollar, another appeared in its place. He was overjoyed that he would never be poor again, and kept on extracting dollars.
>
> Several days later he was found lying atop a huge pile of dollars, dead from thirst and exhaustion. This is the "happiness" of acquisition, the insatiable bottom line.

The pursuit of the bottom line is indeed insatiable. Instead of fulfilling oneself, which can result in true happiness, one may constantly try to be someone else, never satisfied with what one can make of oneself, looking only to outside sources for happiness.

The magic purse was a futile resource and could not gratify an insatiable desire.

Once a young man consulted me. Like the man with the purse, he was perpetually dissatisfied, only he was dissatisfied with who he was. This young man was completing the first of three years in radiology residency, but was dissatisfied with this area of medicine. He was thinking about either psychiatry or pathology, and wanted my opinion about which to choose.

I thought, "That's strange. Psychiatry or pathology? You couldn't possibly think of two more opposite specialties. Psychiatry requires intense interpersonal relationships, whereas pathology requires none at all."

The young man went on to say that prior to radiology he was in an internal medicine program, but he was not happy with that. This aroused my suspicion. I asked, "Before medical school, were you in any other field?" He told me that he had started engineering, but had dropped it because he was not pleased with it.

"How did you manage to stay in medical school?" I asked.

"My family would have killed me if I had quit," he said.

The poor young man, talented as he was, could not learn to find satisfaction in himself, and instead sought the magical solution of the "right" career. He was like the character in another of my mother's bedtime stories, one that taught the futility of trying to magically become someone else.

There was once a stonecutter who earned his living hewing slabs of stone from a mountain. He often bewailed his sorry fate. "I have to work from dawn to dusk, breaking my back lifting this heavy pickaxe all day, and then I barely earn enough to put bread on the table for my family."

One day he heard a loud clamor. Climbing to the peak of the mountain, he could see from afar a parade in the city. The king was in a royal procession, and people had lined the streets, shouting "Bravo! Long live the king!" as they threw flowers at the royal coach.

The stonecutter raised his eyes to heaven. "Dear Lord," he said, "You are a just God. That king and I are both human beings. Where is the justice that he should be so mighty and powerful, and I should be so downtrodden? If You are indeed just, You will give me the opportunity to be mighty as the king."

Suddenly, he felt himself transformed. God had answered his prayer. He was the mighty king, receiving accolades from thousands of loyal subjects. How thrilling it was to be so powerful! Soon, though, he began to feel very uncomfortable. Clad in his ermine robe, he was wilting as the sun's rays fell upon him. "What!" he said. "The sun can humble a king? Then the sun is most powerful. I wish to be the sun."

He was transformed into the sun, and enjoyed its unequaled power. But then he found himself frustrated. A dark cloud had passed beneath him and was blocking his rays. "What!" he said. "A cloud can frustrate the sun? Then it must be more mighty than the sun. I wish to be a cloud."

As a cloud he took great pleasure in frustrating the sun, but then a sharp gust of wind blew him away. "The wind must be mightier than a cloud. I wish to be the wind." As the wind, he became ferocious, causing tidal waves and leveling forests. But suddenly he was stymied. He had encountered a tall mountain that resisted his strongest gusts. "If a mountain is mightier than the wind, I wish to be a tall mountain."

As a tall mountain he dwarfed all else on Earth and felt most

*powerful. But then he felt a sharp pain. A stonecutter wielding a
pickaxe was tearing away parts of him. He said, "If a stonecutter
can dismantle a mountain, then he must be even mightier than
the mountain. I wish to be that stonecutter."*

And so he became the mightiest of all: a stonecutter.

I told the young doctor this story and said, "If you can be
happy with yourself as a person, then you can be happy as an
engineer or whatever kind of doctor you choose to be. If you
are not happy with yourself, you can exhaust all the medical
specialties and all the professions in the world and you will remain dissatisfied."

Our infantile mind wants only what delivers pleasure. If
we remain stuck in that mind, we remain dissatisfied. And
just as we can expect too much of a career, we can expect too
much of material things.

The futility of expecting material possessions to bring
happiness was evidenced by a man who was referred to me
because of suicidal ideation.

"My father is crazy," he said. "He is eighty-five and has built
a multi-million-dollar empire. If he lives to be 200, he cannot
possibly consume more than a fraction of his wealth, yet he
goes to the office every day to make more money. What for?
My share of the family fortune is more than I can ever consume. I have a condo on the West Coast and a condo on the
Riviera. I have a stable full of horses. When I get on a plane,
it's not to go anywhere, but rather to get away from wherever
I am. I don't see any purpose in living."

I said, "With that money at your disposal, just think of the
way you could be helpful to many thousands of people."

The man looked at me quizzically, as if I had just de-
scended from Mars. "Give it away? Why would I want to give
it away?"

This is the ultimate in crass materialism: the loss of purpose in life.

On the other hand, when Baron Rothschild was asked how much money he owned, he cited a sum that was a fraction of his wealth. He said, "The figure I quoted was what I have given to charity. That amount is truly mine and can never be taken from me. Everything else I own is mine only today. Conceivably, I could lose everything tomorrow."

Think back to the "magic purse" story. The insatiability of material desires is in every way similar to addiction. The poor person who is found dead atop a pile of dollars is the drug addict who dies of an overdose. Spiritual values, too, may be insatiable, as in the case of a person who thirsts for knowledge and is forever trying to learn and improve. But the insatiability of spiritual pursuits is never fatal, and whereas the addict is never happy with pursuit of the high, the person engaged in self-improvement and self-fulfillment can be happy in his personal growth. It has been aptly said: "Happiness is not a goal; it is a journey."

Caring for others and giving of oneself for the betterment of total strangers is a uniquely human trait, and when one shares with others, one fulfills oneself. A spiritual person can enjoy material success, but it is not essential: she can also be happy without the ephemeral pleasures in which some people indulge.

Discovering the Nucleus of Self-Respect

Although much of my psychiatric practice has focused on treating alcoholism and drug addiction, I have found that these conditions can serve as models for other situations in which a person's behavior is self-defeating. I firmly believe that low self-esteem is a major factor in most psychiatric problems, and that if a person achieves a feeling of worthiness, one can cope with many of life's challenges.

I have been asked to what I attribute my success with these difficult problems. My answer is that I believe in the basic good and worthiness of every person. I only have to convey my feeling about people to them. What a thrill to see people discover the good in themselves!

Whereas short-term bottom-line thinking is appropriate only for some business situations, there is another "bottom" phenomenon that is more promising: it can actually lead to self-knowledge and transformation. This is the "rock-bottom" phenomenon that so often empowers a person to recover from destructive addictions.

In my forty-plus years of treating people with alcoholism and drug addiction, I have met many people who were so devastated by their addiction that they felt totally worthless, yet were able to find the answer to their question, "Who am I?" in their recovery. One patient helped me see how this occurs.

I was in my second year of psychiatric training when I began counseling Isabel, a recovering alcoholic. When I met her, Isabel was sixty-one. In our first session together, she mesmerized me with her life story. She was one of three daughters of an Episcopalian priest. Isabel began drinking late in adolescence, and at twenty she was drinking very heavily. She married and had a child. When the child was three, her husband said, "Make your choice. It's either the booze or the family."

"I knew I could not stop drinking," Isabel said, "and I wasn't much of a wife or mother. It was only decent to give him the divorce he asked for."

Her husband got custody of the child. So, twenty-eight years old, free, and unattached, Isabel began serving as an escort to some of Pittsburgh's social elite. She acquired a beautiful apartment, the latest in fashions, and all the alcohol she wanted.

After five years, the alcohol began to cause behavioral changes in Isabel that made her undesirable company for her clientele. She then began serving a lower socioeconomic clientele, and she very rapidly deteriorated. Soon she was living in fleabag hotels and prostituting.

Every so often, Isabel was found passed out and taken to a hospital for detoxification. She then attended the hospital's Alcoholics Anonymous meeting, but upon discharge promptly resumed drinking. In fact, over the course of nearly twenty years, Isabel had been detoxed at least eighty times!

Isabel's family was horrified by her behavior and disowned her. Her phone calls to her sisters were answered with a brusque, "Don't you dare call me again" and a hang-up.

Eventually—and on her own—Isabel approached a lawyer who had helped her out of some alcohol-related jams. "David, I need a favor," she said.

"Good God!" the lawyer said. "Not again! What did you do this time?"

"I'm not in any trouble," Isabel said. "I want you to put me away in the state hospital for a year." At that time, Pennsylvania statutes included an Inebriate Act, under which a chronic alcoholic could be committed to a state hospital for "a year and one day." This law had been used by families who wanted to get a chronic alcoholic out of their hair. No alcoholic had ever voluntarily asked to be put away for a year.

"You don't know what you're asking for," the lawyer said. "You're crazy."

"If I'm crazy, then I really belong there," Isabel said. She continued to press her request, and the lawyer finally took her before a judge and had her committed.

After a year of sobriety, Isabel left the state hospital and promptly went to an AA meeting. Someone gave her a few nights of shelter, and she soon found a job as a housekeeper for a renowned physician who was now retired and was himself a chronic alcoholic. Many times Isabel had to lift him off the floor and put him in bed.

Nevertheless, the doctor still sat on the boards of several foundations and was periodically called to testify at Senate hearings. Isabel would receive a call from the doctor's children: "Dad has to be in Washington in two weeks. Get him into shape." Isabel would detox the doctor, get him a haircut and shave, and put him on the plane to Washington. "Now don't you drink on the plane or in Washington," she'd say. "When you come back tomorrow, I'll be waiting for you." The doctor obeyed like a well-trained puppy.

Remember, I was just beginning my career as a psychiatrist. I had never heard anything like this before. My first career was as a rabbi, and seminary did not teach me anything about alcoholism. Medical school was no better. I learned much about some rare diseases but nothing about the most common disease a doctor encounters. In my psychiatric training I was learning much about mental illnesses, but alcohol and drugs were never mentioned.

I was fascinated by Isabel's story. As a fledgling psychiatrist, I knew that there had to be motivation for a person to seek help. What could possibly have motivated Isabel to take so drastic a measure: committing herself to a state mental hospital by a court order? I had to discover her reason, so I told her to come back in a week for another session.

In the next session I heard some more interesting stories. Fascinated but still clueless about her motivation, I had her come back the following week. To make a long story short, I saw Isabel once a week for thirteen years. One night, at age seventy-four, she died peacefully in her sleep.

What was the secret of Isabel's motivation to hospitalize herself? Isabel never directly revealed why she had done so. I was left to my own devices to guess at it, and here is what I think.

Do you know how a volcano is formed? Deep down at the core of the earth lies molten rock that is under extreme pressure. Over many centuries, this lava slowly rises, then makes its way through fissures in the earth's crust to the surface. Once it breaks through the surface, the lava erupts.

I believe that at the core of every human being is a nucleus of self-respect and dignity. We sense that we are unique human beings with much self-worth. For a variety of reasons, this nucleus may be concealed and suppressed, lying somewhere in our subconscious mind, and we may behave as though we are not dignified. Like the lava, this nucleus seeks to break through the surface and be recognized. Once it breaks through into a person's awareness, one may feel, "I am too good to be acting this way. This behavior is beneath my dignity." I think this is the "spiritual awakening" to which the Twelfth Step of AA refers.[1]

Isabel must have been tormented for years by the question "Who am I?" and anesthetized herself with alcohol, but in recovery she found her answer, and in the many years that she helped others in recovery, she implemented her spirituality.

Discovering Our "Nucleus of Worthiness"

If Isabel introduced me to the field of alcoholism and drug addiction, Avi was one of the reasons I remained there.

A number of years ago, I began a small rehabilitation

program in Israel for ex-convicts who had been imprisoned for drug-related crimes. In a session with the first group of clients, I pointed out that we have a natural resistance to avoid damaging an object of beauty. Inasmuch as everyone knows that drugs are damaging, why don't users have a stronger resistance to taking them in the first place? The reason, I told them, was that they had never considered *themselves* to be worthy and beautiful. I said that long-term recovery depends on developing self-esteem, so that one would not want to damage oneself.

One of the ex-convicts said, "How can you expect me to have self-esteem? I'm thirty-four years old, and sixteen of those years have been spent in prison. When I get out of prison, no one will give me a job. When the social worker tells my family that I will be released in ninety days, they are very unhappy. I am a burden and an embarrassment to them. They wish I would stay in jail forever or even die. How am I supposed to get self-esteem?"

I said to him, "Avi, have you ever seen a display of diamonds in a jewelry store window? Those diamonds are scintillatingly beautiful and worth hundreds of thousands of dollars. Do you know what they looked like when they were brought out of the diamond mine? They looked like ugly, dirty pieces of glass, scraps that anyone would think worthless.

"At the diamond mine, there is a *mayvin* (expert) who scrutinizes the ore. He may pick up a 'dirty piece of glass' and marvel at the precious gem that lies within. He sends it to the processing plant, and it emerges as a magnificently beautiful, shining diamond.

"No one can *put* any beauty into a dirty piece of glass. The beauty of the diamond was always there, but it was concealed by layers of material that covered it. The processing plant removed those layers to reveal the beauty of the diamond. They did not *create* the beauty; they just exposed it.

"I may not be a *mayvin* on diamonds, Avi," I said, "but I am a *mayvin* on people. You have a beautiful soul within you, but it has been covered with layers of ugly behavior. We will help you get rid of those layers and reveal the beauty of your soul."

Avi stayed in the program for several months, then in a transitional facility for eight months. After leaving, he found a job and remained free of drugs.

One day, Annette, the administrator of the rehab program, received a call from a family whose elderly mother had died, leaving an apartment full of furniture for which they had no use. They offered to donate the furniture to the rehab program. Annette called Avi and said, "I have no way of getting that furniture here. Could you help us?" Avi assured her that he would get a truck and bring the furniture.

Two days later, Avi called Annette. "I am at the apartment," he said, "but there is no point in bringing the furniture. It is old and dilapidated."

Annette said, "I don't want to disappoint the family, Avi. Bring it here. Perhaps we can salvage some of it."

Avi loaded the truck and brought the furniture to the facility. As he dragged an old sofa up the stairs, an envelope fell from the cushions. It contained 5,000 shekels—about 1,800 dollars. Apparently no family members knew about this money, and the rule of finders-keepers could easily have been applied, especially by someone who used to break into a house for ten shekels.

Avi called Annette and told her about the money. "That's the family's money," she said. "Call them and tell them." The family graciously donated the money to the rehab program.

On a subsequent visit to Israel, I met Avi at a function hosted by the program, and that is when Annette told me the story about the 5,000 shekels. I said to Avi, "Do you remember our first meeting, when you wondered how you could ever have self-esteem? I told you that there was a soul, a beautiful diamond within you. Many people who never stole a penny would have simply pocketed the money. What you did was truly exceptional and shows the beauty of the diamond within you."

Several months later, Avi donated a bronze plaque and affixed it to the door of the rehabilitation center. It read "Diamond Processing Center."

Why have I stayed in the addiction field? Because I like to expose beautiful diamonds. Stuart and Sybil are two more cases in point.

Stuart was admitted for treatment after a serious suicide attempt. He felt he had nothing to live for. His family had left him, and he repeatedly ignored warnings from his law firm partners that his drinking was intolerable and that he would be terminated if he did not stop. He had made some costly errors and caused much embarrassment to the firm by his behavior.

"What do I have to live for?" he asked me. "I don't have my family, I don't have my job, I've made a fool of myself. Live, for what?"

I said, "Do you remember last week's news story, about a gunman who sprayed bullets in a restaurant and killed eight people?"

"Yes," Stuart said.

"What do you think about a person who would kill people he didn't know?"

"He must be crazy."

"Do you really know yourself?" I asked.

Stuart hesitated and bit his lip. "I guess not," he said.

"Then committing suicide would be killing someone you didn't know, right? Are you that crazy?"

Stuart remained silent.

"Tell you what," I said. "I want you to stay for treatment and get into a course where you will get to know who you are. That will take about four years. After that, if you still want to kill yourself, we can discuss it."

Stuart followed a prescribed recovery course. Four years later I received a letter from him saying, "It's been four years since we first met. I have gotten to know myself, and I have no intention of killing myself. My wife is pleased with the new person I have become, and we are considering getting back together."

Stuart discovered who he was.

Sybil was admitted for heroin addiction. She was a registered nurse who had not worked for six years because of her addiction. The reason she came for help was that she had used up all her veins and had none left for injecting heroin.

In the first interview, I noticed that she was wearing a locket. "Is that real gold?" I asked. When she answered in the affirmative, I asked, "How come you still have it and did not sell it to get heroin?"

"I'll never sell this," she said. "This was my mother's."

"Let me see it, please," I said. Sybil handed me the locket, and I took the scissors lying on the desk and made as though I was going to scratch the locket.

"What are you doing?" Sybil said.

I said, "Don't get upset. I'm just going to scratch it up a bit."

"But that's mine," Sybil said.

"I promise I'll give it back to you," I said.

"But I don't want it scratched up," Sybil said. "It is beautiful and very valuable to me."

I said, "So, if something is beautiful and very valuable, you don't let it get damaged, right?" I took Sybil's arms, which were marked by the unsightly tracks and scars of abscesses. "Can you read what that says?" I asked. "It says, 'I am not beautiful. I am not valuable.'"

Tearfully, Sybil said, "I never thought I was any good."

Sybil recovered from her drug addiction and became very active in helping other nurses with drug problems. She discovered that she had a desire to help others. Now Sybil knew who she was.

Many people give up on themselves because they do not know who they are. When they discover who they really are, they gain a self-respect that allows them not only to go on with life, but also to achieve happiness.

You Are Special

Know this: you are someone special. This awareness is particularly important when economic circumstances threaten to subvert your self-esteem, and may make you ask yourself, as Elly did, "Without a job, who am I?"

How we value humanity may influence how we feel about ourself. When the media reports that hundreds, thousands, and even millions of human beings are being killed, that news may decrease our sense of value as a human being. And conventional social standards do not help too much, because our society often ascribes our value to our financial wealth. Permit me to reflect on something I feel is social folly: looking up to people because of their wealth or popularity. This anecdote illustrates that trap.

A man consulted a psychiatrist.

"What is your problem?" the psychiatrist asked.

"I don't have any problems," the man answered.

"Then why have you come to consult me?" the psychiatrist asked.

"Because my family thinks there is something wrong with me," the man answered.

"What is it that your family thinks is wrong?" the psychiatrist asked.

"They think I'm crazy because I love pancakes," the man said.

"That's absurd!" the psychiatrist said. "There is nothing wrong with loving pancakes. Why, I like pancakes myself."

The man's eyes brightened. "You do?" he exclaimed. "Then you must come to my house. I have trunks full of them in my attic."[2]

We will readily agree that this man is mentally ill. Pancakes are something one eats. Collecting pancakes as if they had a value other than to serve as food is insane. Why, then, do we think that a person who has thirty billion dollars and tries to increase his wealth is mentally healthy? Money is a means by which we may acquire the needs and even the luxuries of life. When we have so much money that we couldn't exhaust it even if we lived for five hundred years, what is the point of striving for more money? In what way does that differ from collecting pancakes? Money is a means of acquiring things—or of giving. When superfluous money is not used for those purposes, it is like stored pancakes. However, society has decided that storing pancakes is insane, whereas storing money is not, and we are subject to society's values.

Popularity is like money. As far as fame is concerned, can one really envy the stars of the media and Hollywood? Many of them live most miserable lives, and despite the glitter with which they are showered, they are really pathetic people. Wealthy and starlit people are seen as special, but that is not the kind of specialness that I am advocating.

Nor is social prominence a reliable measure of specialness. When I was in medical school, we were confronted with the fact that we might have to allocate limited medical resources. We were asked, on what basis should we prioritize?

There may be a relative scarcity of resources. Suppose only one artificial kidney is available, and two patients need it. One is a person who has been a welfare recipient for many years and has not contributed anything to the community. The other is a leading citizen, a prominent businessman, treasurer of the church, a family person who is active in many community services. One might reason that the latter person, who does much for the community, deserves the artificial kidney, and on this basis, he is given the kidney.

Six months later, this prominent citizen abandons his family, empties the church treasury, and runs off with another man's wife. Should he now be taken off the kidney? Our conclusion in medical school was that if all the medical conditions are equal, the ethical principle is "first come, first served." *We cannot assign a value to human life on the basis of circumstances.*

If one believes that human beings are created to serve a purpose, then every person is special, and every person has a mission to fulfill. Ethically, every person is special, and one's economic or social status has no bearing on one's value.

We all have the ability to be the finest people we can be, and it is this uniqueness that gives us value as human beings. Even if we have not actualized ourselves, we have the potential to do so. Finally, if we do not accord value and respect to every person, we create a slippery slope that can lead to disastrous consequences.

Whatever one's circumstances may be, every human being is special—and we want our uniqueness to be seen and appreciated.

CHAPTER 5

Coping with Anxiety

OF ALL OF LIFE'S EVENTS, few things generate as much anxiety as losing a job. In addition to the challenge of supporting ourself and our family, loss of a job is a severe blow to the ego, even if the loss is in no way our fault. In fact, although it may be illogical, we may experience job loss as a threat—even a threat to our very survival.

Why? Human beings are endowed with a physiological mechanism to deal with a threat to survival. This is the flight-or-fight reaction, the body's response to an attack, when survival depends on either subduing the assailant or fleeing to safety.

A number of physiological changes occur when we perceive a threat. Understanding these may help us better understand and cope with anxiety.

When we are threatened with danger, the heart rate increases sharply, in order to supply oxygen-carrying blood to the muscles. The respiration rate increases, too, as we inhale more oxygen and dispose more quickly of carbon dioxide. The blood supply shifts from the digestive tract to the muscles where it is most needed. The blood is diverted from the body surface to minimize blood loss from wounds. (This is the reason for pallor.) The liver discharges its store of glucose to provide nutrients for the muscles. The blood now can coagulate more quickly, to minimize hemorrhage. The pupils of the eyes dilate. The blood pressure rises as adrenaline and cortisone-like hormones are secreted into the bloodstream.

These physiologic changes help the body respond effectively to an acute physical assault, whether by a beast, human assailant, or other physical threat. They enhance the body's ability to run away or to defend. In many cases, the confrontation between the attacker and victim is of brief duration. Within a few moments, one has either successfully fled, subdued the assailant, or been killed.

But the human psyche may perceive a variety of threats as an acute attack. A serious threat to one's financial well-being or an assault on one's ego is taken as an attack, and this may trigger the physiologic changes of the fight-or-flight reaction, just as if one were being attacked by a saber-toothed tiger. *However, in this case, they are not effective adaptations.* There is no safe haven to which one can escape, and there is no assailant to defeat. Using the fight-or-flight adaptation to kill an attacking animal eliminates the threat, but punching the CEO in the nose does not. Furthermore, the anxiety is not over in a few moments. To the contrary, it may persist throughout the day and night, for weeks, for months. These persistent but nonadaptive bodily reactions may exert great stress on the body and may result in physical as well as psychological disorders.

In addition to cardiovascular effects, diabetes may develop, the immune system may be inhibited, the inflammatory response may be sluggish, abdominal fat increases, aging accelerates, memory and learning are impaired, and in children growth may be inhibited. (Make no mistake. Children feel the stress of the economic crisis.)

It is, therefore, vital that we find ways to reduce anxiety. I know what you are thinking. "Get me a job. Enable me to support my family the way I was accustomed to, and I won't have anxiety." How I wish I could do so. But we cannot live with wishful thinking. Reality is what it is.[1]

Substances and Anxiety

It is only natural to seek relief from anxiety, but we must do so cautiously. We live in an age with little tolerance for delay: we have jet flights, microwaveable meals, instantaneous news reporting, instant messaging, and cars that accelerate from zero to sixty in 6.3 seconds. So when we are anxious, we not only want relief, we want it fast. So we may think that a drink can do the trick, and so can a tranquilizer.

But beware! The relief from chemicals is transient, a few hours at the most, and when it wears off, the anxiety is back, so you have to take another drink or pop another pill to get the good feelings back. The nature of all relaxing chemicals is that before long, the body gets accustomed to them and they no longer have the same effect. If you depend on a chemical for relief, there is only one thing you can do when it stops working: increase the amount you drink or the number of pills you take. This pattern often escalates beyond a person's control, and many people end up with serious addiction to alcohol or tranquilizers—and the anxiety they were medicating is even worse. This is also true of most sleeping medications. As unpleasant as insomnia may be, the addiction to sleeping medications is worse. Sleeping medication should be used with great discretion, and only under a doctor's supervision.

A number of people reach for another drug, caffeine, when under stress. This may seem a bit strange, because caffeine is a stimulant rather than a relaxant. But many people who feel worn down by stress, especially if they're experiencing insomnia, enjoy the surge of energy that comes from caffeinated drinks. However, this surge will almost inevitably be followed by fatigue, which will lead to more caffeine and the vicious cycle of addictive use.

Some of us react to crisis by turning to an age-old tranquilizer: *food*. For many people, sugar has an effect similar to the brain's own "feel-good" chemicals, dopamine and endorphins. When these people feel the discomfort of anxiety, it is difficult to resist getting relief from something as close as the refrigerator. Just remember that weight is easy to put on, difficult to take off. Eventually, we will emerge from this economic recession, and opportunities for work and savings will return—but if we've compromised our health, we may find ourselves ill prepared to take advantage of new opportunities.

It might help to reflect on one of the reasons for this financial mess: people looking for a quick-fix way to get rich were blinded by that desire and did not see the disaster they were creating. By drinking, popping pills, or eating to "feel good"—numbing the discomfort of anxiety for the short term—we gain only a brief, quick-fix relief from stress, one that may actually threaten our health for the long term. You might not think that you're harming yourself by sitting in front of a big-screen TV indulging in salty and sugary snacks.

Sure, it may momentarily keep you from stressing over another day without work or enough money; but the next day is sure to come, and it will come with both your body and spirit less prepared to cope with it.

Easing Anxiety

A safe anti-anxiety habit—and one of the healthiest things you can do no matter what your financial circumstances—is to exercise. Exercise strengthens the heart, increases lung capacity, burns body fat, regulates blood sugar, builds muscle and bone strength, and boosts the effectiveness of the immune system. Over and above these important functions, exercise is a mood elevator. Exercise has been shown to release endorphins, the body's natural painkillers, and also enhance the mood-lifting neurotransmitters norepinephrine and serotonin.

Aerobic exercise has been shown to be an effective antidepressant medication. It costs nothing, need not be exotic, and there are no side effects. Brisk walking, dancing, cycling, swimming, rowing, racket sports, ice skating: all are excellent anti-anxiety agents. Find a pair of comfortable walking shoes, stock your portable MP3 player, strap it on, and enjoy your walk. Working out with a family member or buddy can keep up your motivation.

An additional bonus to exercise is that it shows you can control some part of your life; it builds self-esteem through the rewards of discipline. One of the devastating effects of the economic meltdown is that we can feel ourselves to be like feathers in the wind, blown in all directions, helpless and powerless over our own fate. A friend told me that when he heard and saw the disaster of the World Trade Center collapse on 9/11, he went into his garden and did some weeding. "I just had to do something I could control."

Gardening is a superb stress reliever. I find that there is something special about seeing life grow from the ground. I could have bought a truckload of tomatoes with what I've spent on growing my own, but the truckload would not have given me the thrill of watching the tomatoes develop. And flowers can be as gratifying as vegetables: the reward of having the gorgeous colors you grew decorate your dinner table will more than reward your effort.

Other hobbies, too, can provide a healthy channeling of emotion and energy and build self-esteem: think of woodworking, bird-watching, or knitting. So do artistic expressions such as photography, painting, writing, or learning to play a musical instrument. You don't have to do work of professional quality to have the pleasure of producing something that expresses your personality, tangible proof of a unique self more valuable than your earning power. Just be sure you don't create more stress by setting your standards too high and treating your hobby like work, rather than having fun and just enjoying the process.

The benefits of meditation as a way to deal with anxiety have been well documented. More methods are available to us now than ever before in history, as an Internet search will prove. Some of them actually combine physical exercise with mental concentration.

One of these, yoga, is an ancient, time-tested way to relax. What used to be seen as an exotic religious exercise from the East has become so widely practiced that many corporations now offer on-site yoga classes for their employees. There are many varieties of yoga, all of which can have a beneficial effect. You might want to sample several classes before deciding which one suits you best. Out of a job, you can still use the public library to find DVDs and books that will help you learn yoga.

Another effective stress reliever that combines physical activity and mental concentration is T'ai Chi. It was originally developed in China as a self-defense technique, but because of its nonaggressive approach emphasizing intelligence over force and its graceful movements, it is more commonly practiced now for its positive effects on both body and mind. T'ai Chi employs a series of positions said to move energy throughout the body, creating an attitude of relaxed readiness. It is easily adaptable for older people who fear falling, or people with physical disabilities. One woman who had trouble doing meditation in traditional sitting postures found that T'ai Chi allowed her to move and meditate simultaneously. She said that T'ai Chi is great for people "with ants in their pants."

The traditional forms of sitting meditation involve either focusing your thoughts on a mantra or other word, an affirmation, or an image such as a candle flame or a picture of a spiritual teacher and simply counting your breaths and allowing your thoughts to pass through your mind without judgment.

You might be a bit apprehensive about trying any of these meditation techniques. You may doubt that they can help because you don't believe it's possible to relax under your dire circumstances. Or perhaps you feel that you shouldn't be wasting your time meditating when you need to be dealing with "practical" issues. But you *have been* meditating! In your brooding over what's happened to you, you have been meditating and using your imagination, but you've been doing so negatively, conjuring up worst-possible scenarios. The great physician Sir William Osler, quoting Thomas Carlyle, said that the words that helped him lead a worry-free life were

"Our main business is not to see what lies dimly at a distance, but to do what lies clearly at hand."

If the meditation techniques I've described seem too difficult or esoteric, you might try one of my favorite methods, creative visualization, which is easy and accessible to just about anybody. Creative visualization simply means to hold a positive, relaxing image firmly in your mind and to make that image your point of focus.

Here's how it works. Find a few minutes when your home is quiet, or go to a peaceful place outdoors. Sit comfortably, relaxed but not slumped, so you can breathe freely. You may play some soft, relaxing music. Take several deep breaths. Relax your muscles. You're not going to do anything now, so you can just let your muscles go flaccid.

Begin with imagining a relaxing scene. Perhaps it is an enjoyable vacation experience, like sunbathing on the beach or lying in a hammock on a pleasant, warm spring day. You may want to create a scene that you'd like to experience: just make it relaxing and enjoyable, with no tension. If you're out of work or in a stressful job situation, try imagining yourself at a new job in a positive setting, doing something that is rewarding and personally satisfying. See the surroundings and see the other employees, friendly and supporting. Savor the feeling of enjoying being at work and earning a living without the stress of worrying about your salary or being fired.

You know that there have been recessions in the past, and we have emerged from them. You know we will emerge from this one, too. Your scene of being at work again can be a reality, not a mere fantasy, and holding that positive thought in your mind can actually help you achieve it.

If you can't conjure up images or relax at first, don't give up. That's normal: like anything new, it may take some practice to get good at it. Try doing the exercise for fifteen minutes upon awakening and fifteen minutes before bedtime—or anytime during the day when you find your anxiety is taking over. Beware of letting your negative thinking undermine your efforts: if you find yourself thinking, "This better work, or else!" that's a negative thought that works against you. It's likely that you've been immersed in negative thinking for a long time, and it will take time to adopt a new perspective.

As you develop a more positive attitude, you will find yourself not only feeling optimistic but actually succeeding in improving things. Remember, just a tiny bit of light can banish a great deal of darkness.

Finding Balance

Everything in life has a purpose, and when anything is used for the purpose for which it was designed, it will serve its natural function in life. However, if you have unrealistic expectations of something, making excessive demands of it and placing a greater burden on it than it was meant to carry, your life will fall out of balance. This is the case for people who have staked too much of their identity on their career or material things. If one has demanded that a job or stock portfolio answer the question "Who am I?" then of course one reacts with fear and anxiety when the "answer" is taken away. Just as exercise and meditation can reduce anxiety, so can the restoration of balance.

The human body requires adequate nutritional input for optimal function. Nutritionists tell us that for optimum health, one must have a balanced diet of proteins, carbohydrates, and fats. A diet top-heavy with only one type of food may provide the requisite number of calories, but it does not provide the essential elements that the body requires.

The human psyche, too, requires adequate emotional nutrition for its optimal function. This is also true of emotional "nutrients." Deprivation of emotional input can have negative consequences on a person's emotional and even physical health. For example, research by René Spitz showed that infants who were not adequately cuddled in the first six months of life failed to thrive and had severe depression.[2] At any phase of life, a certain amount of emotional input is necessary for emotional health. There are various sources: family, friends, work, literature, art, music, hobbies, religion, and so on. These combine in varying proportions to equal the 100 percent of emotional input each person requires. For example, the chart here shows the various components of one person's total emotional input.

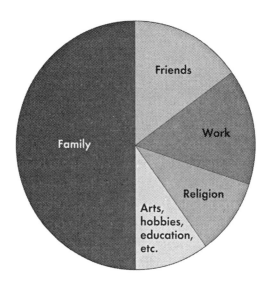

The distribution may vary, but the job should not be expected to fulfill more than 25 percent of a person's emotional needs. The lion's share of input should derive from meaningful interpersonal relationships and *non-work-related* sources. This thesis is confirmed by the work of Boston psychologist Rosalind Barnett, who found that both men and women in good relationships withstood workplace stress better than people without that support.[3] And, according to psychologist and career coach Barbara B. Reinhold, 89 percent of working mothers reported that their parenting experiences made them more effective at work.[4]

The goal of work is primarily to provide one with a livelihood. Of course, work also has an emotional component when one takes pride in one's accomplishments and productivity.

Suppose that a person has few, if any, family ties. He may have no family or may be detached from his family. He may have few close friends. His interest in religion and the humanities is limited. This person may have inordinately high expectations of work, i.e., that in addition to providing a livelihood, *it should provide the lion's share of his emotional needs.* But work is not designed to do that, and calling upon work to do so much is a sign of a life out of balance. When a job plays too great of a role in life, and a person loses that job, depression may result.

If a job has accounted for 25 percent of our emotional well-being, the loss will be difficult, but we will still have 75 percent of our emotional resources to rely on. But if the job accounted for 50 or even 75 percent of those resources, the experience will be devastating, and depression or anxiety may occur.

Part of the solution is to restore balance. Make a list and study your sources of emotional input: family, friends, community, religion, hobbies, meditation, exercise, and so on. Strengthen those that you can, and consciously seek new ones. Make connections; use your extra time to volunteer and thereby to contribute to the world's well-being. Worry less about the future and think more about what you can do today to contribute.

A person who does these things may still feel very sad about the loss of her job and financial security, but she will find other riches in the gifts of *belonging*, of *worthiness*, and of her *competence* as a friend, a community member, and as the kind of person who in small ways helps to make the world a better place. Such a person can fill up the 50- or 75-percent loss with new emotional inputs. And when that person eventually returns to work, she will no longer expect her job to carry such a big load.

CHAPTER 6

Coping with Grief and Depression

REMEMBER THE FIRST-GRADE STORY about Chicken Little? When an acorn fell on her head, she panicked and ran to tell everyone that "the sky is falling, the sky is falling!" If you've lost your job, home, or retirement savings, certainly more than an acorn has fallen on your life—but nevertheless, the sky is *not* really falling.

My work in the past forty-plus years has been treating people with alcohol addiction. I have counseled people who seemed totally ruined, but were able to bounce back to a happy and productive life because they had a glimmer of hope. They taught me something that's crucial for facing hardship: *never despair!* Despair is our worst enemy because it takes away every bit of motivation to survive and recover. When one despairs, one may do some very foolish things, such as casino gambling hoping to avoid losing one's home, or borrowing money from loan sharks to keep a child in college or pay bills. Step number one is "Keep your equilibrium. *Don't panic.*"

We can be confronted with hardships that appear to be overwhelming at times. Yet, if we reflect a bit, we will recall that we have weathered challenges in the past that we had thought were overwhelming, yet we survived. Recalling our strength and resiliency in past difficulties can give us some of the courage and confidence we need to cope with the present.

I have never yet walked away from an Alcoholics Anonymous meeting without taking something valuable along with me about overcoming adversity. An alcoholic shared the following story at one meeting—a story with true antidepressant power.

> *I have been sober for four years, and I wish I could tell you that things have been good. My company downsized; I lost my job and haven't been able to find another job. My wife divorced me and took custody of the children. I was unable to pay the mortgage, and they foreclosed on my house. Last week the finance company repossessed my car. But I can't believe that God brought me all this way just to walk out on me now.*[1]

A woman in recovery from addictions shared another story with me.

> *I am a rabid football fan, and my team is the New York Jets. I will never skip watching a game. One time I had to leave town for the weekend, and I asked a friend of mine to record the football game on her video.*
>
> *When I returned, my friend gave me the video cassette, and said, "Oh, by the way, the Jets won."*

I began watching the game, and the Jets were falling far behind. By half time, they were trailing by 20 points. At other times, I would have been pacing the floor, wringing my hands, and possibly raiding the refrigerator. However, I was perfectly calm, because I knew that my team was going to win, hence there was no need for me to worry.

Ever since I turned my life over to God, I know that it is going to turn out good. There may be some hitches on the way, but I know that God will not fail me.

Sometimes I feel like I am trailing by 20 points at half time, but since I know that the end will be good and that I will overcome and succeed, nothing ever upsets me as it did before.[2]

Someone said that at times like this we should remember that there have always been times like this. We can't give in to despair, and sometimes it's a simple matter of mustering the strength to do whatever we can *just for that day.*

The department store magnate J. C. Penney was asked what was the secret of his success. "Adversity," he said. "I would never have amounted to anything had I not been forced to come up the hard way."

When I came across the following little moral tale, at first it seemed downright foolish.

A man was being chased by a tiger, and he came to the edge of a cliff. He jumped and grabbed hold of a grapevine that protruded from the cliff. Then he saw that beneath him there was another tiger. So he plucked a grape and ate it.

I finally really understood this story during the first Super Bowl Sunday after the fall 2008 financial meltdown, when it struck me that among the many millions of people who watched the game on TV, there had to be thousands who had lost their jobs and were certainly profoundly unhappy—and yet, there they were, watching and enjoying the game. They cheered when their team made a touchdown and were discouraged when the other team did. They were eating a grape while suspended between two tigers.

Gratitude

While there is no denying the severity of the hardships we may be experiencing, we can still find daily enjoyment and gratitude. I recently had a lesson in gratitude. I had just bought a new car, fully loaded, and was very upset that the cruise control was not functioning properly. That day, a woman who was eight months into recovery from alcoholism stopped by to tell me about her good fortune. "I found an apartment that I can afford. Now that my son is going to school all day, I can take a full-time job. I might save enough money to get my car fixed," she said.

"What's wrong with your car?" I asked.

"It doesn't have a reverse gear," she said.

"How do you drive without a reverse gear?" I asked.

"You just have to be careful where you park," she said. "At least I have a way to get around—there are some people who don't even have a car."

I felt pretty meek—instead of being grateful that I had a fully loaded new car, I was griping because the cruise control was not precise!

It may seem like a cliché, but it's really true that we can always find things for which to be thankful if we just try to think positively. It is unfortunate how often people get into the habit of focusing on the negative rather than on the positive. When an instructor returns the test paper, the wrong answers are the ones checked off. Why not check off the *right* answers? We have to switch our perspective.

Here's a good example.

A man on a business trip to Las Vegas visited a casino and placed a two-dollar bet at the roulette table. His number won, and he had a phenomenal winning streak, accumulating 50,000 dollars in winnings. He had the urge to bet just one more time, and went back to the roulette table, where he lost the whole thing.

Back in his hotel room, his wife asked whether he had bet. "I sure did," he said. "How did you do?" she asked. "Not too bad," he said. "I lost two dollars."[3]

The fact is that this man was just two dollars poorer than before he entered the casino. He could have grieved a 50,000-dollar loss, but decided to look at the reality. He actually was out only two dollars.

Learning to practice gratitude is a part of the way we get back up when we've been knocked down. In the process, we begin to switch our perspectives on our *self*. And this gets back to our earlier discussion on self-esteem. What you really are in life is a *person:* a son, daughter, brother, sister, friend; maybe a father, mother, husband, or wife; and above all, *a self*—an identity that often gets lost amid the activities of daily living. Your essence is not altered by adverse economic conditions.

I'm not claiming that it's easy, especially when under stress, to maintain a good feeling about ourselves, to feel worthy over and above what we earn. My epiphany about this occurred in Hot Springs, Arkansas, where I had gone for vacation after being under constant stress, day and night, as medical director of a 300-bed psychiatric hospital. While at Hot Springs, I wanted to take advantage of the mineral baths, touted as a miracle cure for my chronic back pain.

I was ushered into a small cubicle and I immersed myself in a whirlpool bath of nature's own hot water. This was paradise! I was beyond the reach of patients, family members, doctors, nurses, social workers, and probation officers. I was at peace, being soothed by the swirling hot water.

After five minutes, I alighted from the tub and told the attendant that this was pure heaven. "If you want the treatment, you must stay in the whirlpool for twenty-five minutes," he said. I returned to the tub, and after five minutes, I said, "I've got to get out of here." "If you leave now," the attendant said, "you forfeit the treatment." Reluctantly, I returned to the tub for fifteen minutes of agony. Paradise had turned into hell!

This was a rude awakening. I had tolerated uninterrupted stress for three years, but I could not tolerate paradise for more than several minutes! Something was radically wrong.

I consulted a psychologist, who pointed out that if you ask people what they do to relax, they might say, "I curl up with a good book," or "I listen to music," or "I do needlework," or "I play golf." These are all things they *do*, whereas pure relaxation means *not doing* anything. What many people describe as "relaxation" is really "diversion." One's attention is diverted to the book, the music, the needlework, or the golf ball.

"In the whirlpool," the psychologist said, "you had no diversions—nothing to look at, nothing to listen to, no one to talk to, nothing to do—and without any diversions, you had nothing to focus on except yourself. Apparently you must not like yourself very much if you cannot be comfortable in your own company."

This incident set me on the road to the psychology of self-esteem. I believe that many people, like I was, are not pleased with themselves, and are diverted from focusing on themselves by either work or pastimes.[4]

Here's a way to test your self-esteem. When it's quiet in your home, sit back in a comfortable chair, pull the shades, turn off the TV and any other sound equipment, close your eyes, and do nothing other than breathing. After a few minutes, many people—my old self included—feel that they must get up and do something. The more genuine self-esteem you have, the longer you should be able to relax comfortably without any diversion. If you can't sit for at least ten or fifteen minutes, this should be a wake-up call to explore how comfortable you really are with yourself.

With practice—through exercise, through meditation, through hobbies, through the intentional practice of gratitude—we can ease anxiety and sadness and simultaneously build self-esteem. While none of these "cure" the external condition of hard economic times, they help us endure them and find the good in our experiences (as did the man who won 50,000 dollars and lost 50,002 dollars).

And this is how we cope with the depression we may face. It is how we pick ourselves up when we've been knocked down.

When Depression Calls for More than Self-Help

The loss of a job is usually an occasion for sadness or even grief; such feelings are natural with any loss. But there is a difference between grief and clinical depression. In either case, a person feels sad. In grief the sadness is normal, generally improves over a period of time, and usually does not cause despair and disrupt functioning. But in clinical depression there is not only sadness but also self-deprecation and hopelessness.

The loss of a job, home, or savings can understandably result in a grief-like reaction, primarily because in any of these cases, one may not be able to sustain one's lifestyle. But in the case of a layoff, if one's ego is primarily wrapped around one's work, the grief may progress to clinical depression. This may be a reason why the reaction to loss of a job might exceed the norm.

Just as changes in the body chemistry can affect the function of the heart, lungs, and kidneys, they can also affect the function of the brain in a way that prompts severe depression. This can result in a number of symptoms, such as loss of interest in activities, unprovoked crying, loss of appetite and sex drive, insomnia, despair, and death wishes. The person not only has feelings of worthlessness, but may also feel that "I never amounted to anything and I never can amount to anything. I am a burden to my family." These feelings can even lead to suicide attempts.

With this type of depression, there is little another can do to boost the person's self-esteem. It is like trying to get a blind person to see the colors of a rainbow. This type of depression usually requires pharmacological treatment to correct the chemical changes in the body that caused the depression.

These chemical changes can be instigated by anything that upsets the body chemistry, such as surgery, a severe viral infection, or premenstrual or postpartum hormonal changes. They may also occur as side effects of some medications. If they occur without any evident cause, they are thought to be of genetic origin. Excessive stress and insomnia may cause clinical depression, so that the "Who am I?" identity crisis brought on by economic problems or job loss may result in more than an attitudinal depression.

If any of the symptoms of clinical depression occur, psychiatric consultation should be sought. Support and encouragement may not be enough to combat the effects of these chemical changes.

Depression can be a confusing word. In informal use, it often refers to a mood of dejection. But it is also used as a diagnostic term, as in "She has a depression," which refers to what is known in lay language as "clinical depression" and in psychiatric terminology as "major affective disorder." Even more confusingly, a person can be depressed without having "a depression," as when one is sad because of the death of a loved one. Moreover, one can have a clinical depression without having a sad mood. In fact, in severe depressions a person may have no feelings at all, not even of sadness, and cannot cry. Rather, the person is numb, unable to concentrate, and has no interest in anything.

Depression: The Three Types

It may help to distinguish the three types of depression. The first is the sadness of grief, when one has sustained a loss or experienced adversity. This sadness is normal, and is generally resolved by "Doctor Time." (As it is said, "Time is a great healer.") Empathy and emotional support from family and friends are very helpful in making the adjustment to the loss. Pure grief does not require medical treatment. Sometimes, well-meaning family members, wishing to relieve the relative's grief, will get a doctor to prescribe a tranquilizer. But the tranquilizer may numb the person's feelings, not allowing her to proceed with the grief work that is necessary to adjust to the new reality. Much later, this person may have emotional symptoms due to unresolved grief. People who are grieving a loss need handholding, not medication.

A second type of depression is the "depressed personality." This is the person who goes through life chronically discontented. He seems to look at the world through dark glasses. Nothing brings him lasting happiness. In contrast to grief, nothing has happened to warrant his sadness, and one cannot point to the beginning of this sadness. "He has always been like that, even as a child, always moping." This is an attitudinal problem, often related to low self-esteem. Antidepressant medications do not alter this person's attitude. Psychotherapy may help give this person a better perspective on life and elevate his self-esteem.

The third type, which is referred to as "clinical depression," is a medical disorder, due to malfunction of the neurohormones and neurotransmitters that conduct messages within the brain. The most common symptom of clinical depression is profound dejection, and on careful questioning, the person may describe the dejection as being due to an absence of feelings. "If I could cry, I would feel better." There is frequently insomnia, early morning awakening, loss of appetite, loss of interest in things, loss of sex drive, inability to concentrate, and feelings of hopelessness. The latter are responsible for suicidal ideation.

This upset of the body chemistry may result from a variety of causes. Early in my psychiatric training, I myself experienced the symptoms of clinical depression, and when I consulted one of my professors, he asked, "Are you taking any medication?" I told him that I was taking an over-the-counter medication for hay fever. He said, "Stop the medication and let's see what happens." I did so, and within several days the depression lifted. This medication, like many others, may have a side effect of upsetting the body chemistry, resulting in depression.

As we've already noted, body chemistry may also be altered by a viral infection, by surgery of any type, by anesthesia, by premenstrual or postpartum hormonal changes, or by physical exhaustion. Severe stress may upset body chemistry. Mood disorders may also be of genetic origin. In contrast to the depressed personality, someone who has "always been like that," clinical depression generally has an onset. "I felt fine until about three months ago."

Clinical depression often responds to antidepressant medication. There are a variety of these medications, and there is no way of predicting which will benefit a person. A drug that worked miracles for Alice may do nothing for Jane. It may take several weeks to be effective, and one may have to try several before finding the one that provides relief.

Distinguishing the three types of depression does not clear up the confusion, because they may occur in combination. A person with a depressive personality who would not normally be helped by medication may develop a clinical depression for which medication is necessary. A person in grief may experience stress and insomnia, which may result in the chemical upset of a clinical depression.

Here's a key point about antidepressants versus tranquilizers. The antidepressant drugs work by correcting the chemical imbalance. Their effect is not immediate, and they may have to be taken for a long time—but they are not addictive.

Tranquilizers, on the other hand, do not correct the chemical imbalance but, like alcohol, provide quick comfort by depressing the brain. Most tranquilizers can be addictive, and if one depends on them for weeks, serious addiction may result.

The person who feels depressed because of being laid off is experiencing a grief-type reaction. With emotional support, he can adjust to the new reality and look for ways to reestablish himself. If he happens to be a depressive personality, chronically unhappy with the world, his grief reaction can be more severe. It is also possible that the worry itself, especially when it causes stress and insomnia, may trigger a chemical upset resulting in clinical depression. While antidepressant medication will not restore a lost job, clinical depression must be identified and treated properly so that the person can have the energy to weather the crisis and look for other options. It may be necessary to consult a psychiatrist to determine what the nature of one's depression is and what should be done to best relieve it.

CHAPTER 7

Coping with Powerlessness

FORTY-PLUS YEARS of treating people with alcohol problems have provided me with some insights and understandings that have much broader application. In fact, they can even be helpful to anyone adjusting to our current economic crisis.

One of the fundamental problems of the alcoholic is that *he lives in a delusional world.* We must grasp this concept, because one cannot make a proper adjustment to reality if one's perception of reality is faulty. Nor can one achieve happiness with such a distorted perception, unless, of course, the distortion is so absolute that one lives in a fantasy world and has no ties with reality whatsoever. The psychotic who believes himself to be the emperor of China may indeed be happy even if he has to rummage through trash cans for food. Nothing distracts him from his grandiose delusion. However, a person who lives within reality but is delusional in one or more ways is likely to be very unhappy and may have many difficulties in life.

The typical delusion of the alcoholic is that *he can control his drinking.* Like any other delusion, this one is refractory to logic and reasonable argument. Indeed, the definition of "delusion" is a fixed idea that does not yield even to factual disproving. In my psychology course this was illustrated by the case of a person who believed that he was dead, and no one could budge him from this absurd belief. Finally, one psychiatrist asked him, "Do dead men bleed?" "Of course not," the man said. "Good," the psychiatrist said. "I want you to repeat one hundred times, 'Dead men don't bleed.'"

The man did as he was told. When he was finished with his one hundredth recitation, the psychiatrist pricked his finger with a needle, causing him to bleed. The man exclaimed, "Dead men *do* bleed!"

That is the nature of a delusion. The alcoholic may be confronted with repetitive, irrefutable evidence that he cannot control alcohol, but he is obstinate in his denial of this fact. Neither the heartrending appeals of his wife and children nor his repeated arrests for drunk driving have any impact. This denial is overcome only by a crisis—the experience of hitting rock bottom. Rock bottom is highly variable and may range from a rather mild adversity to a catastrophic occurrence, but when it is experienced, the resistance falls away and the alcoholic relinquishes his delusion, coming to terms with the reality that he cannot control his use of alcohol.

There is reason to believe that the inability to control alcohol may have genetic and physiological roots; it doesn't simply indicate a "weak personality." Nevertheless, the alcoholic often sees this as such, which accounts for his fierce resistance to relinquishing the delusion of control.

In fact, people who wield a measure of power in various aspects of their lives may be particularly resistant to accepting that they cannot control their drinking. In *Substance-Abusing High Achievers*, I pointed out that CEOs, doctors, lawyers, nurses, athletes, and other people who exercise control in their daily lives may have more than the average resistance to accepting that there is this one aspect of their behavior that they cannot control.[1]

What is remarkable is that once the alcoholic relinquishes his delusion of control, he may begin a character transformation that extends far beyond his abstinence from alcohol. A person who was self-centered, opinionated, self-righteous, inconsiderate, and arrogant may develop character traits that are the polar opposites of his previous personality. None of these changes could occur as long as he persisted in his delusion of control. Why relinquishing this delusion is so pivotal in character transformation is unclear, but this principle is the basis of all Twelve Step programs for addiction, wherein the person must accept his or her inability to control this aspect of behavior. The Twelve Step program is a structured approach to identifying and correcting various character defects.

It appears that a person may feel that *being in control is part of one's identity;* hence, accepting one's inability to control may be seen *as a threat to one's very existence,* which may account for the intense resistance to yielding the delusion of control.

Prior to the marvelous advances of modern technology, control may not have occupied so prominent a role in a person's thinking. Think of how our sense of control has grown in our daily lives. When I was a child, I pushed a toy car along the floor. Today, a three-year-old gleefully maneuvers a car across the room by remote control. One can call home before leaving work and turn on the oven by remote, and operators in the space center can control the movements of a spaceship millions of miles away. Unprecedented degrees of control have become part of everyday life, and we may fail to see the boundaries where control ends.

It is of interest that other instances of accepting one's inability to control are not likely to result in character transformation. Survivors of tornadoes or earthquakes or those who have lost loved ones to incurable diseases are certainly aware of their inability to exert control over these facts of life. But no one expects to be in control of nature, and the vulnerability to the vicissitudes of nature is not taken as an indication of personal failure. The personality of a survivor of a natural disaster may, therefore, be unchanged. It is different when one believes that one can and should control one's life; in this case, loss of control is perceived as a threat.

How does an addict's loss of control relate to the current situation? We come now to today's crisis, the economic meltdown. Obviously, losing one's job amid massive layoffs should not be seen as a personal failure, nor should the erosion of one's savings be taken as a lack of investment acumen. However, this is where logic fails to carry the day. Perhaps because we train for a job, pursue the acquisition of a job, and expect the continuation of our job to depend on our performance, we develop the delusion that we can control our employment, and we may take the job loss as a personal failure and a sharp blow to our ego. Because this aspect of control is associated with one's identity—as noted earlier, we may be more human *doings* than human *beings*—the person may well wonder, "Without a job, who am I?"

If, like the alcoholic, we can accept that this aspect of our life may not be entirely subject to our control, we may not only avoid a severe depression, but, like the alcoholic whose relinquishing the delusion of control allows the development of a finer character and a pursuit of happiness, we may find our life much more productive and much happier.

People with low self-esteem are particularly likely to strive for power and control, because dominating others soothes their feelings of inferiority.

I can recall my elementary school teachers. Many of them loved to teach. They took pleasure in our gaining knowledge, and we loved them. But I recall one teacher who was mean. The kids hated her because she wielded her authority over them arbitrarily, meting out unfair tasks and keeping kids after school. I shared the kids' dislike of her, but in retrospect I feel sorry for her: her self-esteem was so low that in desperation she had to dominate helpless kids to feel better about herself.

Anytime our self-esteem suffers, we may seek to compensate by increasing our control. The economic crisis and layoffs have delivered a crushing blow to our feelings of power, rendering us utterly powerless without any avenue for appeal. People whose self-esteem depends heavily on their ability to work and earn may feel pulverized, and they may try to bolster their sagging self-esteem by wielding more control over others. Inasmuch as family members are most readily available, there is a danger that intrafamilial relationships may deteriorate as a result—which may further aggravate the laid-off person's pain.

Being alert to this possibility is the best way to defend against it. Increasing our love for family members and taking even greater interest in each other can forestall toxic control.

If we appreciate the emotional as well as the financial impacts of the economic crisis, and if we recognize how great a role the desire for power plays in our lives, we are in a position to alter our perspectives and develop a healthier concept of human value. If we succeed in downplaying the role of power, we can become more pleasant and more lovable. We are in a better position to enjoy the beauty of the world. We can maximize our self-actualization by developing an attitude toward knowledge and learning that enables us to improve ourselves as human beings and increase our pride in our uniqueness.

Powerlessness

Of course, loss of income is a major setback. We may have plans that have to be scrapped, and we may have to make significant changes in our lifestyle. But there is more to it than that.

Suppose that, for whatever reason, a person finds his job situation intolerable and resigns. He cannot find another job, and his income is curtailed. Yet, though this is a severe stress, it differs from being laid off, because in this case it was *his* decision to leave the job. He called the shot; it did not *happen* to him. In contrast, what the layoffs in the economic crisis have done is made us aware of our powerlessness, and that is a severe blow.

As I see it, there are two prominent qualities in nature: *power* and *beauty*. The eruption of a volcano and the mass destruction of a tornado, hurricane, or tsunami are examples of nature's enormous power. The beauty of nature can be seen in the majestic snow-capped mountains of the Alps, the jungles of Africa, and the breathtaking Grand Canyon. When we feel that we are sharing nature's power, we can appreciate its beauty. When we feel we are impotent, nothing looks beautiful.

We may not be aware of it because it is so pervasive, but we are actually obsessed with power. We strive to invent more and more instruments that will increase our mastery over things. Unfortunately, for many people the quest for power has become a major goal in life, and one may react in unhealthy ways if one feels that one's need for it is frustrated.

Control can be destructive, and the most toxic type is when one uses one's authority or position to control other people. The tragedy is that it is invariably counterproductive, because no one likes being controlled, and control breeds resentment.

Control can lead to abuse, as when a spouse tries to dominate a partner or when parents try to control their children. These are relationships where there should be a bond of love, but the resentment consequent to being controlled can significantly encroach upon and erode the love. Of course, children require discipline, but when a child reaches the age of reason, discipline should be rooted in parental respect and love rather than in authoritarian control. And if a marriage is one of mutual respect and a desire to please the partner, there is no need for domination.

Our obsession is indicated by the popular aphorism "Knowledge is power." The true value of knowledge is that it fulfills the spiritual dimension of increasing one's awareness of the world, rather than simply serving utilitarian purposes. Knowledge of Plato's dialogues or the Shakespearean plays is intrinsically edifying. Inasmuch as this kind of learning is unique to human beings and is not shared by other living things, it elevates one's humanity, even though it does not increase one's power.

Dr. Rachel Naomi Remen says, "We are a culture that values mastery and control, that cultivates self-sufficiency, competence, independence. But in the shadow of these values lies a profound rejection of our human wholeness . . . In a highly technological world, we may forget our own goodness and place value instead on our skills and our expertise. But it is not our expertise that will restore the world. The future may depend less on our expertise than on our faithfulness to life."[2]

Blame

It is generally said that there are three absolute essentials for life: (1) food and water, (2) clothing, and (3) shelter. From what I've observed, I think there is a fourth essential: *someone to blame.* When we feel that power and control have been taken from us, we seek a culprit to blame for our powerlessness.

Understandably, there is much discussion about who is at fault for the current economic recession. Who are the culprits? Irresponsible bankers, CEOs, the head of the Federal Reserve System, greedy market manipulators, credit card companies, the president? All of the above?

Okay, you've found someone to blame. Now what? That doesn't get your job or home back for you, nor does it restore the value of your investments. It does give you someone at whom you can vent your anger, but that's about all it does, which is not much of an accomplishment.

If blaming someone doesn't accomplish anything, why is it so widespread? From childhood on we blame others. "She made me do it." "He started it—he hit me first." And as we grow up, we may become more sophisticated in blaming, but essentially it's the same thing.

The reason blaming is so common is that it serves a purpose. As long as we can find someone to blame, it gives us a reason *why we don't have to make changes in ourself.* "It's his fault. Let him make the changes." This is an erroneous way of thinking, but it seems to provide a person with comfort and with justification for continuing to live as one has been living.

Ultimately, we are going to have to make some radical changes. We have been living in an era of prosperity, and our inclination to spend is further fueled by the purveyors of goods. Our philosophy is to spend money, and if we don't have it, then we borrow in order to spend. We do this as individuals, and we elect people who believe this as well.

Habits are difficult to change. Our children absorb our way of thinking, and lecturing to them is not going to impress them. They will learn only by example.

We would like to punish the villains whose recklessness has caused this economic meltdown. If we could determine who they are and punish them, we would be free to go on living as we had been. That's the psychological gain of blame.

The false comfort of blaming can cause a person to come up with the most ridiculous fault-finding—and yet consider it to be perfectly logical. If we continue to make excuses for things that go wrong, they are likely to occur over and over again. George Washington Carver said that "ninety-nine percent of the failures come from people who have the habit of making excuses."

If we can recognize the futility of blame, we can make some valuable changes in many aspects of life. We don't have to blame our husbands, wives, children, elected officials, or anyone in society. Rather, we can look at what we can do to make things better for ourselves.

Envy

As self-defeating as blame is the "deadly sin" of *envy*. Many people still have jobs and are earning well. Your neighbor may be fortunate in that his job is secure. In fact, he has just vacationed in Tahiti, while you are struggling to make ends meet.

You might wonder, "Why me? Why are others more fortunate, while I don't know how I can keep my home?" (Incidentally, someone said, "When a sorrow comes, we have no right to ask, 'Why did this happen to me?' unless we ask the same question for every joy that comes our way.") Envy is a foolish trait. It accomplishes nothing, while it is spiritually very depressing. As Proverbs 14:30 puts it, "Envy is the rot of the bones."

A rabbi told me that one of his parishioners had complained of chronic envy of his neighbor. "He just bought a new luxury car, while mine spends more time in the repair shop than with me."

The rabbi said, "Doesn't your neighbor suffer with stomach ulcers?" "Yes," the man said. "There you have it," the rabbi said. "If you want the car that he has, you must accept his ulcers. It comes in a package."

This reminded me of the story my father told me about Moshe and Chaim, who had come to America from my father's village in Hornostipol, near Kiev, Ukraine, and occasionally visited him. Here is their tale:

> Moshe had come to America as a young man and was very enterprising. He started a storefront laundry and eventually developed a very profitable laundry and a linen supply business. Chaim, on the other hand, had a corner grocery and barely eked out a living.
>
> Although Moshe was quite wealthy, he was miserable. He suffered from stomach ulcers, and in those days there was really no treatment for this. Moshe lived on soda crackers and milk.
>
> When they met, Moshe asked Chaim, "So, how are things with you?" Chaim sighed and said, "Not good, Moshe. I have to be up at four o'clock in the morning to go to the market, then I have to stand on my feet all day until nine o'clock at night. And

what do I earn from all this? All I can afford to eat is dark bread and radish."

Moshe said, "Chaim, you are a fool! I would gladly give away both my laundries to be able to eat dark bread and radish!"

In spite of your hardships, you have much for which you can be grateful. Don't be envious of those who seem to be more fortunate than you. They might gladly trade places with you.

A Collective Wake-Up Call

Our experiences of powerlessness and lost control generate feelings of fear and anxiety, and they bring forth a desire to blame others and to envy what they have. A part of us knows that control and power are illusions, and knows that the urge to blame and the feelings of envy are distractions. But if we treat these negative feelings as alarm signals, they can still be of use. They can be a wake-up call to change.

On more than one occasion, my alarm clock has dutifully awoken me, and I have turned it off to get "just five minutes more" sleep, only to wake up an hour and a half later. More than one alcoholic has similarly relapsed after an effective wake-up call. These alcoholics seem to hit bottom again and again and again, but the delusion of control returns, and the alcoholic resumes drinking until the next crisis. For some, though, a final rock-bottom crisis pushes them to change. They may go to treatment or consistently participate in a Twelve Step program, which helps prevent relapse.

For people caught in today's economic meltdown, the crisis can be like the alcoholic's rock-bottom wake-up call. This wake-up call is signaled by the alarm bells of fear, anxiety, feelings of powerlessness, and urges to control, blame, or envy. And as the alcoholic needs continued involvement in a Twelve Step program to maintain recovery, we will need continued involvement with new actions and thought patterns to change our attachment to our job, our wealth, and perhaps our home. We have to behave differently as we learn that we are more than all of these things.

Obviously, people have *some* control over their economic well-being. We can take actions that likely will improve—or undermine—our financial health. But as the recent recession demonstrates so painfully, our control in this arena is far from absolute.

The current economic crisis will eventually ease, and although we may be scarred, we will go back to work and renew our savings. But beware: we are then prone to relapse into the delusion that we can control our economic well-being, which may seem to obviate making true changes in our lives, rendering us vulnerable to repeat our negative reactions in a subsequent crisis. Under such conditions, we will readily slip back into thinking that we are nothing without a good job and without wealth.

Just what is wrong with our lifestyle, and what kind of changes are necessary?

Two prevalent concepts govern the way many Americans live: *consumerism* and *entitlement*. Like subliminal messages that may influence how we feel, think, and behave, these concepts exert subtle effects that may determine our lifestyle.

To put it succinctly, consumerism is an industry-based trend dedicated to seducing us into wanting things and then making us think that these are actual needs rather than just wants.

When I was a child in the 1930s, air conditioning and television did not exist. When they came into being, they were considered luxuries. Today, they are generally thought of as necessities. Television bombards us with countless items, presented to suggest that without them, our lives are incomplete. A child who desires a particular doll or toy may wail in a way that indicates that without that item, life may not be worth living. Very often, the thrill of the new doll or toy wears off in a rather brief period, and the dearly coveted items can be found in the toy box with other items that have lost their special value. Adults are essentially no different.

One philosopher, upon viewing a display of items in a store window, remarked, "I never realized that there were so many things I can do without." But that was a philosopher, a profound thinker who could see beyond life's superficialities. Most people are subject to the influence of consumerism and can be rather easily convinced that things that promise to add pleasure to their lives will make them happier, and in their pursuit of happiness, these things become necessities.

Let's dwell a bit on this point. The Founding Fathers, in the Declaration of Independence, state that among the inalienable rights of humanity are "Life, Liberty and the pursuit of *Happiness.*" It is noteworthy that they did not say "pursuit of *pleasure.*" In my childhood years (in the 1930s), one could not equate happiness with pleasure, because life was fraught with too much misery to allow a person to consider pleasure to be a realistic goal in life. In the early 1900s—before the advent of antibacterial and antibiotic medications—the average life expectancy in the United States was around fifty.[3] Infant mortality was high, childhood diseases were rampant, and young people died of pneumonia and tuberculosis. Workplaces were dismal and sometimes dangerous. Communication was difficult, and household chores were laborious. Today, the average life expectancy is around seventy-eight,[4] many childhood diseases have been eliminated, jet flight makes distant places accessible in hours instead of weeks, workplaces are quite comfortable, one can communicate with anyone on the planet who has a cell phone or Internet access, and home appliances and convenience foods have taken much of the drudgery out of household work. With so many daily hardships eliminated, it is now possible to think that the goal of life is the attainment of maximum pleasure.

While technological advances have been helping us meet our needs more comfortably, medical treatments have been evolving not only with wonder drugs and unprecedented surgical procedures, but with chemicals that promise to eliminate the anxieties and stresses of normal life. Before 1950, relief from mental anguish could be achieved only with alcohol and sedatives, which worked only by obtunding the brain to the point of drowsiness. In 1955, the first "tranquil but alert" pill, meprobamate, was launched, ushering in the era of "happy pills." Meprobamate was eventually replaced by a number of drugs belonging to the benzodiazepine group. No one suspected then, and many people are unaware even today, that most of these drugs are potentially addictive. Tranquilizers, or "happy pills," are the largest class of medications dispensed in the United States![5]

The motto of one chemical-producing company, "Better life through chemistry," has taken on a new meaning. To many of us, it has appeared that technology and medical science were going to restore humankind to the idyllic Garden of Eden, and the goal of "the pursuit of happiness" was within reach. And even if one could not be euphoric, the elimination of stress and anxiety would allow a person to achieve contentment. This being seen as humanity's destiny, the miraculous achievements of electronics and medicine now seemed to enable us to control that destiny. The desire to believe this was so strong that it prevented people from seeing the fallacies in this concept.

But what is wrong with seeking contentment and freedom from stress and anxiety as a legitimate goal in life?

It was just when I entered medical school in 1955 that meprobamate made its advent on the market. My professor of pharmacology, who knew that I intended to become a psychiatrist, said, "Now we are going to put all you shrinks out of business." I did not see this as a threat. While antibiotics and corticosteroids were going to enable me to treat people with heretofore incurable diseases, the addition of tranquilizers to the medical armamentarium would enable me to cure people's emotional ills. I felt a surge of power.

One day, as I was looking to buy some evaporated milk, I noticed the slogan on one brand: "Milk from contented cows." I wondered, "Why on earth should I be interested in a cow's mental status?" I then realized that the manufacturer wanted to convince me that his milk was superior in quality to his competitors', and this was because his cows were the finest. What made them the finest? Why, they were contented! In other words, the excellence of a cow depends on its degree of contentment. But even if we buy this marketing ploy, do we need to adopt contentment as our own highest goal?

One need not believe in the special creation of the human race to realize that whereas other forms of life are motivated to achieve a maximum of pleasure, humans are designed for something beyond that. Nature does not do stupid things. It endowed the spider with the ability to spin a web and the bee with the ability to make honeycombs of perfect hexagons. Given that the human brain can compose the symphonies of Beethoven, write the plays of Shakespeare, paint the canvases of Rembrandt, sculpt the masterpieces of Michelangelo, and unlock the secret of the atom as Einstein did—does this equip us only to aspire to bovine contentment? The soaring potential of the human mind indicates that nature intended us to have a goal in life far beyond tranquility. Failure to pursue that higher goal and resigning oneself to the pursuit of pleasure or tranquility frustrates an essential human need: to be everything that we can be.

The drug addict is a clear example of how the pursuit of tranquility or euphoria is self-defeating and results in the opposite of sustained pleasure. The body always builds physiological tolerance: whatever amount of chemical it takes to produce the sought-after sensation, the body accommodates to it so that it no longer produces the desired effect, and one must progressively increase the quantity consumed. One eventually reaches the point where massive doses of a drug fail to provide the desired pleasurable sensation: in fact, it only undermines the ability to function.

Many people live under the delusion that they can acquire happiness by increasing their wealth or enjoying various luxuries. Very much like drug addicts, they do take transitory pleasure in these rewards, but it is evanescent, and they soon find themselves bereft of the happiness they sought. They are then driven to find something else that they feel will give them the happiness they seek. Their pursuit is insatiable. Bertrand Russell said, "It has been said that man is a rational animal. I have been searching for evidence which could support this."

Philosophy aside, the half century since the introduction of tranquilizers has shown my esteemed professor to have been wrong. Not only have tranquilizers not replaced psychiatrists, but to the contrary, psychiatrists have added many patients who have developed serious addictions to these drugs. Another prevalent concept is "entitlement." We have come to believe that everyone is *entitled* to the good things in life—in this case, happiness and contentment—whether or not one makes an effort to achieve them. The Founding Fathers never said that happiness is an inalienable human right. Rather, they thoughtfully said that the inalienable right was the *pursuit* of happiness. One must exert effort to achieve happiness. The sense of entitlement, however, asserts that this is not so. It asserts that everyone should be happy and content whether or not one *pursues* these goals. This is not true.

The current crisis may be a collective wake-up call for our consumerist, entitled society. Many supposed certainties have evaporated into thin air. Institutions that were thought to be invulnerable have crumbled like houses of cards. The notion that we can completely control our financial lives turned out to be a delusion. At times like these, we should rethink our values. While job and financial security should remain a high priority, we should realize that we must look elsewhere for true happiness.

Finding Happiness in the Self

The psychiatrist and author Viktor Frankl, who experienced the horrors of the death camps in World War II, has described how everything was taken from him, and he was stripped to the bare skin, facing imminent death. But, said Frankl, there was one thing the Nazis could not take from him: his attitude toward death. He still had the ability to choose how he would face death, and it was this ability that gave him human dignity even under the worst possible circumstances.

We have asked, "Without a job, who am I?" The answer is, "I am a dignified human being who can choose and determine how I will face and cope with adversity. I may have lost my job and I may have lost my investments, but *I did not lose myself.*" But this can be my answer only if I have a sense of self that is independent of the prevailing social values.

"I am a spiritual being," we can claim. "I can be the rational animal that eluded Bertrand Russell. I can contemplate an ultimate purpose to my existence. I can discover my character defects and improve upon them. I can overcome my self-centered animalistic drives. Rather than being a slave to my bodily drives, I can choose right from wrong and act accordingly. I can eliminate my grudges and resentments. I can control my anger. I can forgive. I can relinquish my drive to dominate others. If I choose to be religious, I can develop a relationship with God."

These are some of the unique qualities a person can develop. However, if we are wedded to the "pleasure principle," always subject to the prevailing consumerism and entitlement doctrines, we may find little time and even less motivation to make self-fulfillment our primary goal in life.

Indeed, the shock of the economic crisis may cause us to rethink our values, and through that process we may attain and retain a valid identity.

Doing Good and Feeling Good

I was invited to participate in a tribute banquet honoring a group of volunteers. The group consisted of people of all ages, from older adolescents to retirees. These people donated several hours a week as companions to shut-ins— elderly people who live alone and whose social and physical conditions isolate them from much of the world. The volunteers may take them to shop in the supermarket, to a doctor's office, or just for a pleasant drive. They may sit with them, read to them, or play a game with them. The shut-ins often look forward to the time with the volunteer as the high point of the week.

On the tables at the tribute dinner were brochures describing the group's activities, headlined "Doing Good vs. Feeling Good."

Having spent the lion's share of my career working with alcohol and drug addicts, and realizing that in spite of the many billions of dollars spent on efforts to curb the drug epidemic, we have made virtually no progress in preventing alcohol and drug addiction, I was struck by this phrase. The people I was treating had one thing in common: they were seeking a "good feeling" and found it in alcohol, cocaine, heroin, or other drugs. It is only natural to want to feel good, but the addict turns to a chemical for a "high" that is only momentary and entails many destructive consequences.

But what if we were able to switch our goal in life from "feeling good" to "doing good"? We would likely not turn to chemicals! Furthermore, whereas the high of a chemical is fleeting, the good feeling that results from doing good persists for a long, long time.

There at the tribute banquet, I felt that I had stumbled across the secret of preventing drug addiction. The following day, I met with a group of parents of adolescents who were in our treatment program, and I pointed out to them that if more families established the goal that "What this family stands for is *doing good* in whatever way possible," our youngsters might not resort to drugs.

The following day a therapist told me that the parents had

been impressed by what I had said. He overheard them saying, "Dr. Twerski is right! We have to get our children to do some volunteering."

My heart sank. They had not heard me at all. You don't tell the children to do volunteering. *You do it yourself* and show them that this is an important goal in life. Whether one volunteers to help people; to combat famine in third-world countries; or to advocate for preserving the environment, preventing acid rain, or preventing the extermination of rare species—all these are ways to distract a person from the self-centered pleasure-seeking that can lead to ruinous addiction.

The feeling that results from doing good is edifying, and can greatly elevate one's self-esteem. It can provide a meaningful answer to the question, "Without a job, who am I?" One achieves an identity as a sentient and caring human being.

To "esteem" something means to evaluate it. That is where the term "to *estimate*" comes from. We generally value things for one of two reasons: its aesthetic appearance or its function. Thus, if one has a handsome grandfather clock that is broken beyond repair, one keeps it because it is a handsome piece of furniture. Although it has lost the ability to tell time, it still has aesthetic value. But if a can opener is dull and cannot open cans, one discards it, because in contrast to the grandfather clock, it is not ornamental.

What, then, gives me value (esteem) as a person? The mirror tells me that I am not decorative. Even those people who may be stunningly attractive will eventually lose their beauty. What gives a person value is one's *function*. In order to have self-esteem, a person must know what his or her function is.

Earning a livelihood honestly and supporting one's family is indeed a most important human function, but as we have seen, it is not one's *only* function. We come into the world as selfish little animals, concerned only with self-gratification. With proper parental and social discipline, we mature and master our animalistic drives. We learn how to live moral and ethical lives, and to develop into dignified human beings.

Our animalistic drives never disappear. We all have urges of lust, power, acquisitiveness, and pride. As a child, I remember seeing a man of 103, hobbling with a cane, stoop to pick up what he thought was a coin. The desire for money may stay with a person until the very end.

A major human function, therefore, is to transform ourselves from purely biological creatures to spiritual beings. Here we find our true value, and if, for whatever reason, one cannot earn a livelihood, whether because of illness, disability, or being laid off, one still has the function of developing one's traits to their finest. An answer to the question, "Without a job, who am I?" is we are beings who constantly seek to elevate ourselves above the animal level in every way possible.

CHAPTER 8

A Power Greater than Ourselves

FOR MANY PEOPLE, recognizing their powerlessness in controlling certain aspects of their lives turns out to be a positive experience. Alcoholics in Twelve Step programs are encouraged to recognize "a power greater than themselves" to begin the road to recovery, and this isn't bad advice for people recovering from the devastation that can come with job and financial losses. Each person defines that power in his or her own way; in this chapter we'll discuss three sources of strength and support that many people successfully turn to as that "Higher Power" when they experience powerlessness in some part of their lives. These are (1) the solace of religion and prayer, (2) the support of family and friends, and (3) for people with children, the sense of perspective and balance that comes with placing the children's welfare first.

The Solace of Religion and Prayer

Before becoming a physician, I served as a pulpit rabbi for a number of years, and I preached to people, stressing the importance of faith and trust in God. When I became a physician, I entered into an unspoken agreement that I would not preach religion, just as the clergy would not practice medicine. Therefore, I do not wish to trespass those boundary lines. Yet I cannot ignore the central role of religion and prayer in giving most people in the world their experience of a Higher Power.

Turning to God for help in times of distress or disease often raises the question, "Why ask God to relieve one's distress?" If a person believes that God can do so because He is in control of the world, then He could have prevented the distress from occurring in the first place. If, indeed, it pleased God for the distressing event to occur, why should one now expect Him to undo it?

Various answers to this question have been proposed, but none are fully satisfying. I do not claim to have an answer, but I can share with you a possible solution that came to me in a pediatrician's office.

A mother had brought her baby to the pediatrician for his third immunization. The child was smiling happily, playing with the toys in the waiting room. When the doctor emerged, the child shrieked, recognizing this white-clad person as the villain who on two previous occasions had stabbed him with a sharp instrument and had caused him to feel sick for two days. The child clung to his mother for protection, then kicked and clawed when the mother carried him into the treatment room. We can well imagine what the baby was feeling at this time. "What has happened to my mother who has always loved me and cared for me? Why is she carrying me into this villain's lair for him to torture me again?" The baby's world had suddenly turned upside down. The mother then willingly collaborated with the villain, restraining the child while the villain administered the torture! There is no way the child could make any sense of the mother's betrayal. He could not know that this temporary pain would protect him from dreaded diseases, and that far from being cruel, the mother was acting out of love for him.

No sooner did the doctor administer the injection and leave than the baby threw his arms around the mother, clinging to her for safety. This is baffling! Why was the baby turning to the mother for protection now? Hadn't she just violated his trust by collaborating with the villain? All we can surmise is that the mother's recent behavior did not eliminate the child's trust in her. The baby could not fathom her actions, which were some kind of inexplicable aberration. Nevertheless, she was still the mother of whose love and care he was certain.

The gap between the child's infantile mind and the mother's mature thinking is great. Yet both the child's mind and the mother's mind are finite. The gap between even the wisest human mind and the infinite wisdom of God is much greater, because anything relative to infinity is negligibly infinitesimal.

A person of faith believes that God is the ultimate of goodness and kindness and that He cares for His children with infinite love. As with the baby and his mother, this trust in God is not lost when He allows distressful things to occur. One prays to Him and turns to Him for help. The baby cannot conceive that his mother is acting out of love. We may not be able to understand in what way terrible things could possibly be in our best interest, but at least we can understand that it *could* be so. This has often been referred to as "a leap of faith," and this is why a person in distress may pray to God for help.

Sometimes people of faith are privileged to gain an insight into the mystery of God's goodness. Many people have had experiences that appeared to be unqualified disasters, yet many years later, they recognize them as "blessings in disguise" whose true nature could not be grasped at the time. Of course, we may never understand some events, such as the horrible loss of life in a tsunami or earthquake, but even then, human nature is such that survivors turn to God for consolation, like the baby who clings to his mother.

There is the story of the person who dreamt that he was walking with God, and their feet made two sets of tracks in the sand. Then the person was struck with disaster, and noticed that there was only one set of footprints. He cried to God, "Why did You desert me when I was in distress?" God replied, "No, My child. I did not desert you. You saw only one set of footprints because that was when I was carrying you."

What if a person is not religious and does not believe in God? Is prayer not an option?

At a meeting of Alcoholics Anonymous, the speaker, who was seven years sober, related that on his initial exposure to AA, he rejected the program. "It's all about God," he said, "and I am an atheist." He returned a year later, saying that he realized he needed the program in order to stop drinking—but was there any way he could do so without invoking God? He was told that all he had to do was choose a Higher Power; in fact, he could see the Twelve Step program as his Higher Power. That suited him just fine. Subsequently, he was told that he must find a sponsor to serve as his mentor in sobriety, and he did. The sponsor told him that he must pray every day.

"Wait a minute," he said. "I was told that I did not have to pray to God. I don't believe in God."

The sponsor said, "That's okay. Don't pray to God. Just pray."

"What kind of nonsense is that? How can I pray if I don't believe in God?"

The sponsor said, "Look here, you SOB. Do you want to get sober or do you want to stay drunk? If you want to stay sober, then you pray every day."

"I didn't have much choice," the man said, "so I pray every day. I don't believe in God. But when I pray, that reminds me that I'm not God."

Earlier we noted that the feeling of absolute control of one's life is delusional and may result in a sense of failure when things go wrong, as when one is laid off. The control delusion is essentially a belief that one is one's own God. If prayer reminds us that we are not God and helps divest use of the delusion of control, we may adjust much better to adversity.

Prayer seems to have a mysterious universality. After a community has been struck by tragedy, it is common for people to assemble in prayer, and it is not unusual for nonbelievers to participate. Everyone seems to have a notion that prayer is in some way beneficial.

A visitor to the noted physicist Neils Bohr was shocked to see a horseshoe suspended over his door. "You!" the visitor exclaimed, "The world's leading scientist, and you believe in a good luck charm!" Bohr smiled. "No," he said, "I don't believe in it, but that thing works whether you believe in it or not."

Much the same can be said for prayer. It works even if one does not believe in God.

Prayer can take many forms. There is prayer for *petition* or *intercession*, in which one asks God for something for oneself or for others. There is prayer of *confession*, asking forgiveness for wrongdoing. There is prayer of *lamentation*, crying in distress and asking for relief. There is prayer of *adoration*, giving honor and praise to God, and there is prayer of *thanksgiving*, expressing gratitude. Prayer may be verbalized or silent, individual or communal.

The four principal themes that are found in prayer are (1) gratitude toward God, (2) expressing love of God, (3) admitting one's wrongs and asking for forgiveness, and (4) asking relief from distress. These themes also occur in interpersonal relations, although some people seem to have difficulty with them.

Let's look at gratitude first. You may have observed a mother telling her five-year-old, "Say 'thank you' to the nice man for the candy," and the child responding with a grunt. In adults, there may be resistance to acknowledging gratitude because a person may feel that accepting a favor makes one beholden to the benefactor, but why children are reluctant to say "Thank you" is not clear.

Now let's consider the theme of love. It has been noted that during courtship, a young man and young woman may be lavish in expressing their love for one another. However, once they are married, they may not hear the cherished words "I love you" for the next sixty-five years!

Finally, forgiveness: the resistance to admitting that one was wrong can be truly formidable. It seems to be human nature to defend a mistake and to admit it only when all defenses have been exhausted.

It may be easier to say these three phrases to God than to another human being: "I thank You," "I love You," and "I am sorry, but I was wrong. Please forgive me." But if we say them to God often enough, that may lower our resistance to saying them to another person. I can only wonder how many failed marriages could have been preserved if those words had been exchanged more often: "I thank you," "I love you," and "I am sorry, but I was wrong. Please forgive me."

So, the praying person may have another answer to the question, "Without a job, who am I?" One may say, "I am a person who can pray. I can be thankful and express my gratitude. I am a person who is capable of true love rather than just animal lust, and I am a person who can admit my mistakes, apologize, and try to make amends."

Family and Friends

Family members and friends can be very supportive in softening the crushing blow of the loss of one's job, home, or investments. Recall the *For Better or For Worse* strip: Elly wonders, "Without a job, who am I?" and her little girl embraces her, saying, "Mum!" I was, therefore, taken aback by a call from a man who asked whether he should tell his wife that he had been laid off. He was concerned that this would be too traumatic for her.

I couldn't understand how he planned to manage if he did not tell her. Was he going to lie to her and tell her he was going to work every morning, then hang around someplace all day and continue this practice perhaps for months until he found employment? How was he intending to support the family at their previous level if he was not earning? Did he think his only value to the family was as a provider, and that being unemployed rendered him valueless to them? He alleged that this might be too traumatic for his wife, but I think the truth was that it was too traumatic for him.

Family members should be understanding: in addition to

new financial limitations for the family, the laid-off person may need help in feeling worthy. There is power in words of praise. Compliments can inspire a person to achieve and to deal with the challenges of daily life. People tend to live up to the compliments they receive. It is possible to give praise even in the face of negative acts: find something praiseworthy and speak up about it.

Close friends, too, should be told of a job loss. Depriving oneself of friendship at a time of stress intensifies the suffering. In this economic meltdown, many have suffered layoffs through no fault of their own. There is no reason to feel ashamed, and everyone will understand. If you share this information with close friends, you are not asking them to feel sorry for you. There is some truth in the aphorism that "joy that is shared is doubled, and grief that is shared is halved." In fact, any reduction is appreciated. At any rate, by sharing this information with friends you will avoid the tendency to withdraw from them.

If the recession put you in a position where you need help, be great enough to accept it. Do not allow false pride to deprive you and your family of what you need. Friendships, especially true friendships, are invaluable. There is a legend about a person who slept for seventy years. When, upon awakening, he did not find a single person he knew, he exclaimed, "Without friends, death is preferable!"

A person who is laid off after many years of loyalty to a firm may feel rejected and even betrayed, even though the firm may not have had a choice. Losing one's job is losing a meaningful relationship. This is why strengthening ties of friendship is so important.

Nevertheless, one must be cautious not to lose one's sense of self in friendships. I recall a cartoon by the late Charles

Schulz, creator of *Peanuts*. Two little girls are with Snoopy, and one of them says, "Look at that sad look on Snoopy's face." Snoopy droops his face to accommodate her. The other girl says, "Oh, no! I like a dog with a cheerful expression." Snoopy then smiles with the left side of his face, while still drooping the right side. Trying to please everyone, Snoopy pleases no one, and he must exert much effort to maintain the grotesque facial expression.

That is what happens if a person lacks a personal identity and tries to accommodate everyone's wishes. So listen to others, be respectful of others, but find yourself and be yourself.

Putting Our Children First

In an adult, it may take some type of crisis experience to raise the question "Who am I?" which may lead a person to self-discovery and the formation of a valid entity. Not so with children, all of whom deal with the "Who am I?" issue every day as their identities take shape under the guidance of the adults in their lives.

It's much like the story of the three umpires. The first one says, "I calls 'em as I sees 'em, balls and strikes." The second says, "I calls 'em as they *are*, balls and strikes." The third umpire says, "They ain't *until I calls 'em* balls and strikes."

An adult may have a valid self-concept or an erroneous self-concept. A child has no self-concept and must formulate one, hopefully with the support of caring parents.

Dwarfed by giant adults, children may see the world as a risky and unpredictable place. Therefore, if parents express their stress and preoccupation during a crisis by ignoring or punishing a child, that child won't think, "My parents don't know what they're doing." Rather, the child will think, "I don't understand why I am being punished. I must be bad." In this way, children start to form negative self-concepts. Unwise critical comments may also be taken very seriously, and if a parent, because of her own insecurity, remarks, "You're stupid," the child will believe that is true.

Children need reassurance and positive strokes. We generally "catch" our children doing something wrong, but we often do not acknowledge when they do something right. We should "catch" children doing something right at least three times a day.

As adults, we have a need to be acknowledged. This need is even greater in kids, precisely because they feel so diminutive and helpless. If they are demonstrably loved and appreciated, they are more likely to develop a positive identity. If not, they may grope for *any* identity. We may recall the class clown, who repeatedly got himself ejected from class.

While doing psychological evaluations in a jail, I met one prisoner who had been arrested in a bungled bank robbery. As I introduced myself to him, he said proudly, "Doc, did you see my picture on the front page today?" This young man's father had been a penniless immigrant who worked his way up to wealth and had become a prominent citizen of the community. The son, who felt he could not achieve his father's success, found another way to public prominence: his picture on the front page as a bank robber.

If we are aware that children, like us, wonder "Who am I?" we can learn to see their needs as more important than our own troubles, even in times of crisis. We must try to help them develop a positive identity. The way we feel about ourselves will be conveyed to our children. For them to feel special, we must feel that way ourselves. If we feel rootless, wondering,

"Without a job, who am I?" our children are likely to feel that way about themselves.

Parenting requires preparing children for reality. It is virtually impossible to go through life without any adversities, some of which, like being laid off, can undermine one's self-esteem, and children should be equipped to cope with adversity.

One psychologist said that if you give your children self-esteem, you have given them everything. It is true that self-esteem is one's greatest asset. However, it is a mistake to think that you can *give* your children self-esteem. All you can do is to provide them with the means so that they can build their own.

Children feel special when they sense that they are their parents' central focus. It makes little difference whether one is an only child or one of eight. An only child of parents who are self-centered may not feel special, whereas a child in a large family with devoted parents can feel special.

When a couple marries, each person has particular wants and needs. If these conflict and the conflict is not resolved, the relationship is affected, and the couple can decide how much to do about it.

All this changes radically when they have a child. A child does not ask to be brought into the world, and the world is fraught with challenges and hardships. It is the parents' decision, and the parents, therefore, have *a sacred obligation to give the child the best chances to have a happy and productive life.*

One of the most vital components of a child's emotional health is a sense of security. The child feels this security when the parents have a truly loving and stable relationship. If there are unresolved conflicts between the parents, the child feels that, too. Indeed, the child's security is affected more deeply by parental conflict than by the breadwinner's loss of a job! Children are exquisitely sensitive, subject to emotional impacts long before they can express themselves verbally or even understand spoken language. Children have the same 100 billion brain cells that adults have, and theirs are not yet cluttered with all the material stored in the adult brain; hence they can have a greater receptivity. Adults may rely heavily on verbal language, whereas children are receptive to body language. A child can sense the ambience in the home. Do not think for a moment that you can put something over on a child!

When a couple brings a child into the world, the partners must be ready to yield on their wants and needs for the child's sake. Their behavior may no longer be determined by "what I would like" but by "what is in the child's best interest." By no means does this mean pampering the child. Indeed, discipline may be in the child's best interest, but the parents should fully agree on how to administer it. If parents cannot resolve their conflicts, they should quickly seek competent help to bring them into a truly harmonious relationship.

Self-centeredness is not a laudable trait, but conflict-producing parental self-centeredness is frankly criminal, because children pay the price. On the other hand, when they sense that their parents are truly there for them, children feel special, and this is the greatest gift that parents can give them.

It's also a gift parents give to themselves by fulfilling this responsibility that is "greater than self."

CHAPTER 9

Lemons into Lemonade

YOU MAY BE WONDERING, "Is this person crazy? I've lost my job of twenty-some years with no hope of a job in sight, I can't pay my bills, I can't pay for my children's tuition, and my home may be up for foreclosure. It's the worst possible nightmare, and this guy is talking about making the best of the situation! He must be out of his mind!"

Not for a moment do I trivialize your agony, but let me tell you what I mean by turning lemons into lemonade and finding the good in tough situations. Sometimes pain can reveal what we need most.

In medical school, we learned to examine the patient's eye-grounds—the back of the eye—because this can provide important information about the patient's physical condition. This is a part of a regular physical exam. The physician shines a beam of light through the pupil of the eye, dilating the pupil with eye drops first if necessary. Looking through the pupil, the doctor can see the blood vessels on the retina, and this gives him information about the condition of the blood vessels in the body, how they are affected by high blood pressure, diabetes, and other conditions. It also enables him to determine if there is increased intracranial pressure that pushes out the optic nerve. But there is a risk here. A person with glaucoma—an often symptomless but serious eye disease that can cause blindness—will feel excruciating pain if the pupils are dilated.

The professor warned us about this, advising that we should be ready to immediately administer a dose of morphine to such a patient. "But don't feel bad if this happens, because this reveals that the patient has glaucoma and should be treated for it. Otherwise the glaucoma might have continued without any symptoms, resulting in loss of vision. If you have precipitated an attack of acute glaucoma causing terrible pain, you have actually done the patient a great favor that can save the patient's vision."

Being a victim of the economic turndown may be in the same category. The pain of a layoff or other loss can help reveal an underlying "illness" that we need to heal in order to be truly happy.

We all desire happiness, and we've discussed some of the mistaken ideas about what constitutes happiness. An addict may see it as the numb feeling of alcohol or the "high" of heroin or cocaine. The compulsive gambler may see it as a win at the casino. A wealthy person may see it as negotiating a very profitable deal. But these are illusions of happiness, producing only momentary pleasure. We've also noted that some people feel that happiness is their birthright, and that they are entitled to it without exerting an effort to merit it. And many people plod along, feeling more or less satisfied with their lifestyle, giving little or no thought to whether it can produce true happiness. I have suggested that the trauma of the economic crisis may be a wake-up call to bring us out of our tedium.

A human being is a composite creature. The human body, for all intents and purposes, is an animal body. What makes us uniquely human is "something else" beyond the body. Our biology teachers taught us that man is *Homo sapiens*, which means a primate with intellect. While intelligence is, of course, of great importance, it is not the only feature that distinguishes us from other living things. Earlier, I alluded to a number of human traits, among which are the ability to contemplate a purpose for life, the ability to improve oneself, the ability to make moral decisions, and the ability to give of one's energies and possessions to help others. I suggest that these and other uniquely human traits constitute the *human spirit*, and it is the combination of the spirit and the body that constitutes a human being.

We know that our physical component requires certain nutrients for optimum health and functioning, and that lack of an essential nutrient—such as iron or vitamin C—will result in a disease. These deficiencies can be corrected only by providing the missing substances. Thus, a person suffering from iron deficiency will not improve even if given all vitamins and all other minerals. One must receive iron to correct the condition.

Similarly, our other component, the *spirit*, requires its specific nutrients. If one does not provide the spirit with its essential needs, one develops a "Spirituality Deficiency Syndrome." The symptom of this condition is chronic unhappiness. (This is not to say that a person who suffers from depression, a different condition, is spiritually deficient!) Unfortunately, the person may not be aware of the roots of the unhappiness.

Instead of providing the spirit with its essential nutrients, the person may turn to any of a variety of behaviors, essentially escapist techniques that, like drugs, provide only a transitory relief. Unfortunately, the variety of such maneuvers is legion, so that a person may go through an entire lifetime without having been a truly "whole person," complete in both body and spirit.

Our routine lives, before the economic crisis, may have been such that we never had adequate cause to pause and reflect on whether we were really living to the fullest. Many of us had a Spirituality Deficiency Syndrome but had never been aware of it and come to terms with it. The personal upheaval wrought by the economic crisis may bring us around to assessing our lives not only by our material possessions and physical activities but also by our spiritual involvement. This realization, similar to the attack of acute glaucoma, may be a silver lining to a very dark cloud.

Coping with Adversity

Our economy will eventually change for the better, but until then, we must learn how to cope with adversity. Author Tim Hansel said, "It's not so much what happens *to* us, as what happens *in* us that counts, or what we *think* has happened to us."

In a similar vein, the Serenity Prayer offers universal wisdom that also inspires people in Twelve Step groups of all kinds:

> God, grant me the serenity
> To accept the things I cannot change,
> The courage to change the things I can,
> And the wisdom to know the difference.

Keep this quote and prayer in mind as we consider some stories of people who coped with difficult realities. I heard this first story at a meeting of Al-Anon, a recovery group for people involved with alcoholics or other addicts.

At an Al-Anon meeting, a woman related her story. She had just celebrated her thirty-fourth wedding anniversary. The first seventeen years were fraught with the misery of her husband's drinking. The last seventeen years were of recovery.

"After three years of marriage and not having become pregnant," she said, "I made the rounds of specialists. I was finally told to accept that I would never be able to carry a child. That was difficult to accept, but because adoption was an option, I was able to accept it.

"We adopted two lovely children, and after my husband stopped drinking, we had a happy family. When I turned forty, I decided it was time to give up smoking. I went through several weeks of very unpleasant withdrawal.

"After several weeks of feeling good again, the symptoms returned. I consulted my doctor and found out that I was not in nicotine withdrawal at all. I was pregnant! The impossible had occurred. I had been blessed with a miracle.

"I thought that I had rid myself of all bitterness and resentment, but they returned in a crescendo when the nurse put Jimmy in my arms. He was a Down syndrome child. 'God,' I said, 'why did You do this to me? I had made peace with not having a child of my own. We have a beautiful family with our two adopted children. Why did You deceive me to think I would be happy with a child I carried, and then hit me with this?'

"Every night, my husband and I prayed over the crib. 'God,' we said, 'we know that You can do anything. You have done so many miracles for us. Please, do just one more. Change him.'

"Night after night we prayed for a miracle. Then one day the miracle happened. God changed us!"

The woman continued, "Now, if this child did not come into the world for anything else than what I am about to tell you, it would all have been worth it. Because, when I sit in the rocker holding Jimmy in my arms, and I see his short, stubby fingers, and the way his eyes are, you know, and I know how much I love that child with all his shortcomings, that's when I can understand how much God can love me even with all my shortcomings."

I felt a chill go up my spine. I had never heard the Serenity Prayer articulated so powerfully. They had been praying for the wrong thing! They wanted to change the unchangeable. But God knew what they really needed, and He gave them the courage to cope with this challenge.

You see, there's a theme arising here, about the relationship between adversity and happiness. We must ask the question, can one ever be happy about feeling pain?

A young woman was involved in a terrible automobile accident, sustaining numerous injuries. With the nerves from her spinal cord to her right arm severed, she had no sensation and no mobility in that arm and hand. Her nerves were repaired surgically, but she was told the surgery's success wouldn't be immediately obvious. After several months of healing with her arm in a sling, she would know how much sensation and function would return to it.

One evening several months later, the young woman was playing cards with friends. Holding both her cards and a cigarette in her left hand, she dropped the cigarette, which fell on her right hand. Feeling the burn, she promptly threw the cards in the

air and hopped out of her chair, shouting for joy, "It's hurting!
It's hurting!"

The pain of the burn indicated that her sensation was returning. The surgery had been successful, and she would regain the use of her arm. Under other circumstances, a person who sustains a burn might say, "Ouch!" perhaps accompanied by some expletives. For this woman, the discomfort was transcended by its good-news message, and the pain was more than welcome.

If I had designed the world, I would have left out pain. But I have to admit that discomfort can be constructive. At one AA meeting I attended, the speaker related the misery of his active addiction. Then he challenged the audience with a question. "Can anyone tell me anything they have ever learned from a pleasurable experience?"

I had never thought of it quite that way. I could not think of anything I had learned from a really enjoyable experience, other than to try to repeat it.

Another time, while waiting at the dentist's office, I came across a magazine article titled, "How Do Lobsters Grow?" Come to think of it, how *can* a lobster grow? It is encased in a rigid shell that does not expand. The answer is that as the lobster grows, the shell becomes confining and oppressive, and the lobster feels discomfort. It finally retreats to an underwater rock formation to be safe from predatory fish, sheds its shell, and produces a more spacious one. As the lobster continues to grow, the new shell eventually becomes oppressive, and the lobster will repeat the process until it reaches its maximum size.

What's the signal that it's time to shed the shell? *Discomfort!*

If lobsters had access to doctors, they might never grow. Why? Because when they felt the pinch of the oppressive shell, they would get a prescription for a painkiller or a tranquilizer. With the discomfort gone, they would not shed the shell and produce a more spacious one. They would die as tiny little lobsters.

For human beings, too, discomfort is often a signal that it's time to grow.

Another animal story: at a fishery on the West Coast I had the opportunity to observe wild salmon. Born in rivers, these fish spend most of their lives in the Pacific Ocean, but they eventually make their way back upstream, against the tide, to lay their eggs at the place where they were born. When they encounter a waterfall, they jump up against it. If they don't succeed, they swim around a bit to restore their energy, and they try again and again until they do succeed. If there are two small cascades together, they never try to jump over both at one time.

I was deeply affected by watching these fish. The salmon may not be intelligent. Their drive to get to their spawning place is an instinct, and nothing stops them. If they fail to make a jump, they try again, but they take only one step at a time.

Humans do not have a goal by instinct. We arrive at the knowledge of our goal by means of our intellect. However, once we determine what our ultimate goal is, there should be no obstacle that can stop us. We may have to go against the popular current to achieve our goal, and if we do not succeed, we should not give up. We should keep on trying until we do succeed.

Tommy Lasorda said, "Determination is what makes the difference between the impossible and the possible."[1]

The salmon appear to know this.

Like the salmon, we should not take a bigger jump than we can handle. We should make gradual progress, doing only what is realistically achievable. That's how we can reach our ultimate goal.

Crisis and Opportunity

Someone said, "When you fall down, look around. You may discover something you couldn't see when you were standing up."

Indeed, crisis can create opportunity. If we can avoid negative thinking, we may find opportunities when we're jobless that we wouldn't have found otherwise. A positive attitude and commitment can bring unexpected results.

What is commitment? David McNally said, "It is the serious promise to press on, to get up, no matter how many times you are knocked down." In *Late Bloomers*, Brendan Gill lists numerous examples of people who started and developed lucrative careers after age sixty-five.[2]

Many people have been successful when the odds were against them. I think of the philanthropist who helped me through medical school. He sweated bullets whenever he had to sign a check, which was a laborious task for him. When this man had emigrated from Russia in 1920, he sought employment and applied for a job as caretaker of a small synagogue. He was turned down because he could not sign his name, and this would be necessary if he were to receive deliveries.

So he found work with a man who collected scrap metal and rags, and eventually was able to get his own horse and wagon. A clever businessman, he was soon able to buy a few properties. He survived the Great Depression and made some very successful investments. When I met him in 1950, he was a very wealthy philanthropist.

This man helped pay my medical school tuition. His secretary would write the check, and with great effort, he would sign it. He smiled and said, "Good thing I don't know how to write. If I could have signed my name, I would have become a caretaker of a synagogue and could not help you with your medical school."

Sometimes we may miss an opportunity because our minds are set on doing things a certain way and we resist change. In fact, there is scientific evidence showing that when a person is forced to change a fundamental belief or opinion, the brain undergoes a series of nervous sensations equivalent to torture.[3] It has been said, "The toughest thing to change is our approach to change. Expect change; it is inevitable. Your decision is to decide whether it is to be by consent or coercion."[4] Do you have some valuable ideas, but lack the confidence to try them? Don't be afraid. Remember, a baseball player who has a .300 average makes millions, but he hits safely only three times out of ten! Or think about the following story:

> *Charles Darrow was a salesperson who lived during the Great Depression. When sales positions dried up, he squeezed out a living walking dogs, washing cars and doing other assorted odd jobs. In the evening, he worked on developing a board game that several people could play at once. Darrow had visions of every home owning one of his games.*
>
> *The first company to purchase his idea sold 5,000 games in the first year. Parker Brothers later purchased the game, beefed up the marketing, and today, 20,000 of those games are sold every*

week. Darrow's willingness to pursue new possibilities resulted in
America's favorite board game—Monopoly.[5]

When we are caught up in the routine of work, our minds may not be free to grasp new ideas, or to develop them. An idea that remains undeveloped does not amount to much. That's the lesson of this story: The author of a biography of Samuel Clemens, better known as Mark Twain, traveled to Hannibal, Missouri, to gather information in the great humorist's hometown. He met an old-timer who had known him, who said, "Heck, I knew just as many stories as Sam Clemens. Only difference is that he writ 'em down." Our literature was enriched not because Mark Twain merely "knew" these stories, but because he "writ 'em down."

You may be capable of creativity. Don't sell yourself short. Do something with your ideas. You may be pleasantly surprised. The adversity of the recession may bring out the best in many people. You could be one of them.

Is It Really Impossible?

The economic recession has caused some people to feel that they are trapped in an impossible situation. I've heard it said that the impossible just takes more effort than the possible. That is not quite true. No matter how much effort I put into flapping my arms, I cannot fly like a bird. But too often, when we feel we are between a rock and a hard place, we may see things as impossible when they are actually within our reach.

Being a sports enthusiast, I have found inspiration in several of Dov Lipman's stories in *Time-out.*[6]

For years, it was known to be impossible for a human being

to run a mile in less than four minutes. The record was four minutes, 1.3 seconds, and many physiologists said that this was the physical limit. Obviously, there was no point in trying something that was physically impossible.

Roger Bannister was a twenty-five-year-old medical student who questioned the validity of this scientific "fact." He used intense interval training and his own special techniques in an attempt to break the four-minute barrier.

Reporting on the May 6, 1954, race between British AAA and Oxford University, the Associated Press story records that Bannister "bided his time until about 300 yards from the tape, when he urged himself to make a supreme effort. With a machine-like, seemingly effortless stride he drew away steadily from Chataway [his competitor] and, head thrown back slightly, he breasted the cool, stiff wind on the last turn to come driving down the homestretch to climax his spectacular performance."

Bannister crossed the finish line, and two track officials held him up while spectators converged on him. The crowd was silent until they heard the announcer begin to proclaim Bannister's time. "Three . . ." The cheers of the crowd drowned out the rest of his time. Despite a fifteen-mile-per-hour crosswind, Bannister had run the mile in just three minutes, 59.4 seconds. The four-minute mile barrier had been broken! The world was in shock. The unthinkable, *what was considered to be beyond human ability,* had occurred. Bannister's time was referred to as "the Miracle Mile."

What is most amazing is that just 45 days later, Bannister's record was broken by John Landy of Australia, who ran the mile in three minutes, 57.9 seconds! By the end of 1957, sixteen people had run the mile in less than four minutes. By 2001, 855 people had done so. They had done the "impossible."

It is obvious that some things are impossible because *we see them as impossible*, but if our perceptions change, the impossible becomes possible. We may be absolutely certain that something is unchangeable reality, whereas factually it is not so.

Is it possible for a person born with only one hand to become a baseball pitcher? How about a major league pitcher who pitches a no-hit game? It sounds absurd, right?

Jim Abbott did not think it was impossible. He was born without a right hand. On the pitcher's mound, he wore a right-hander's fielder's glove on the stump of his right arm. While completing his follow-through after delivering a pitch, he rapidly switched the glove to his left hand so he could handle any balls hit back to him. Should he have to throw to a base, he could remove the glove using his other arm while retaining the ball in his left hand—all in one quick motion.

Abbott played for the California Angels in 1988, winning twelve games in his rookie year. In 1991, Abbott won eighteen games with a 2.89 ERA. On September 4, 1993, he pitched a no-hitter against the Cleveland Indians. Abbott would say, "As you learned to play baseball with two hands, I learned to play with one, so it was easy!"

Easy! With dogged determination, not only did Abbott make the apparent impossibility into a reality, but he felt that it was easy!

They Fly Because They *Know* They Can

I've been telling you stories of known "heroes" who have overcome great adversity, so you may be tempted to write them off: *They're special. They have something I don't.* If you are inclined to think this way, consider this. You've seen the scene on TV numerous times: a tornado, flood, wildfire. A couple holds their children in front of the remnants of their home. They have no place to live. Everything they owned, everything they treasured, irretrievably gone.

What happened to those people? If the media were to show us where they are five or ten years later, we would generally find that they are living normal lives, because that's what happens. Although the family is devastated, there is usually some help from neighbors or charitable donations, and parents still have their jobs. After grieving over their misfortune, they gradually return to a normal life.

In another *Peanuts* cartoon strip, Lucy declares, "I can't stand it anymore! I give up!" Charlie Brown says, "Where do you go to give up?" That's the point: there is nowhere we can go to give up.

So even amid our economic meltdown, we know that eventually life will return to normal, although not necessarily to pre-recession conditions. Our primary task, then, is to try to minimize the misery of the interval and to emerge with as few residual scars as possible. A person had no say in being laid off. But to lose a job is one thing, to lose a sense of self, "Without a job, who am I?" is another thing.

As noted, we may become so absorbed in our work and our routine that we do not have time to think about ourselves. We don't ask ourselves, "*With* a job, who am I?" and we allow our job to define us. Being laid off cannot be seen as a blessing, but if losing a job helps us find ourselves, it's not all that bad a trade-off.

In retrospect, we often see that things are not the catastrophes we initially thought them to be. If you've ever had a cinder fly into your eye, it feels like a mountain. When it is removed with a Q-tip, you see it is a barely visible speck. The discomfort was great because it lodged in a very sensitive area. Losing one's job is by no means a tiny speck, yet the discomfort it causes depends on how sensitive we are. I hope that the ideas in this book strengthen our sense of self, which reduces our vulnerability.

Think of the history of boxing: there are numerous records of boxers who were knocked down but arose before the count of ten and went on to win the fight. Strengthening our faith in ourselves and substituting positive thinking for negative thinking can enable us to get up before the count of ten and win the fight.

In my office, I have a poster of birds in graceful flight. The caption reads, "They fly because they think they can." That statement is not quite accurate. It is more correct to say, "They fly because they *know* they can." I doubt that birds think about their ability to fly. If a bird sitting atop a tall tree were to think about flying, it might say, "If I move from here, I'll fall down and get killed." The bird does not think. By intuition, which resides in the primitive brain, it knows it can fly.

Human beings, too, have a primitive brain. That's the part that controls our breathing and other vital functions, and is the seat of our emotions and physical drives. Then humans developed the cerebral cortex, an extremely sophisticated onboard computer—the brain that could develop mathematics, compose symphonies, and write literature. This sophisticated brain was superimposed on the primitive brain, so a person now processes primitive brain ideas through the cerebral cortex—and that has created a problem.

Human beings have many intuitive ideas and skills, but we may not be aware of them. They arise in the primitive brain, but instead of implementing them, we *think* about them. We may be like birds who would think, "I wonder if I could fly by flapping my wings?" Such a bird would never risk flight. Many of our intuitive skills, therefore, lie dormant.

We are so involved in the activities of daily life that we do not give much, if any, attention to our intuitive ideas. It is not unusual, when circumstances change, that our intuitive ideas and skills are recognized and implemented.

Take Grandma Moses, for example, who is considered a foremost American folk painter. She lived the arduous life of a farm wife and did some embroidery. At age seventy-six, she was too frail to do farm work and could not embroider because of arthritis, so she began to paint! Her popular paintings have become classics of their kind. Where was this artistic talent until age seventy-six? Concealed under the daily chores of a farm wife! Grandma Moses lived to 101, and there is good reason to believe that her artistic productivity contributed to her longevity.

Psychologist and philosopher William James said, "I have no doubt that most people live, whether physically, intellectually or morally, in a very restricted circle of their potential being . . . *we all have reservoirs of life to draw upon of which we do not dream.*"

If you've been laid off, of course you should look for opportunities for employment. But I have two suggestions:

(1) Keep an "Idea Book" handy, and write down every idea that occurs to you, even if it seems zany. Review your book from time to time to see which ideas may be realistic, then try to implement them.

(2) Don't be deterred by rejections. Think of Evelyn Gregory, who applied for a job as a flight attendant at age seventy-one. After being rejected by three air-

lines, she got a job as a gate agent, and six months later was hired as a flight attendant—a job she held for seven years.

One day at the post office I ran into a judge I knew. He told me that he had just been accepted to medical school, at age fifty-nine!

We may hesitate to implement an idea because we think we are not good enough at it. Here are some wise words: "It is better to do something imperfectly than to do nothing flawlessly." Henry Drummond, a nineteenth-century British politician, said, "Unless a man undertakes more than he can possibly do, he will never do all he can do."

In the past, you may have had ideas that you have since discarded. If you were to write your autobiography, you would probably recall some earlier plans that you never actualized. Take another look at them. You may have the opportunity to do so now.

For too long, many of us have neglected knowing ourselves. We haven't corrected our shortcomings and maximized our strengths. Having fallen prey to unwarranted feelings of inadequacy and unworthiness, we did not develop our interpersonal relationships with our spouses, children, relatives, and friends. Many of us have paid lip service to religion, failing to benefit from the enormous treasury of wisdom in the world's great faiths and to develop a meaningful contact with God.

In forty-plus years of psychiatric practice, I have met many people who were not at all in dire economic straits, but were unhappy with themselves. Their family lives often left much to be desired because they did not fulfill themselves in a number of ways.

I know that history, literature, music, and art will not put food on the table or pay utility bills. Of course we must search for ways to improve our economic status. But in addition to that, we should make an effort to improve ourselves in every way possible. The economy will eventually turn around, and our financial conditions will improve. Don't be lured into the ennui of limiting your identity to your job or financial status. Let your "primitive brain" emerge from its layers of concealment, and let your intuition enrich your life.

The rewards of true self-fulfillment await you—but you must be willing to begin the task of uncovering your own "nucleus of worthiness." I wish you the best in your journey of discovery.

Notes

Chapter 1

1. Clara S. L. Brenner, "Family Mealtime," *U.S.News and World Report*, October 27, 2004, http://health.usnews.com/usnews/health/briefs/childrenshealth/hb041027a.htm.

Chapter 2

1. Ernest Jones, *The Life and Work of Sigmund Freud* (New York: Basic Books, 1953).

2. John Bradshaw, *Healing the Shame That Binds You*, rev. ed. (Deerfield Beach, FL: Health Communications, Inc., 2005).

3. Liz Carpenter, "Getting Better All the Time," quoted in Glenn Van Ekeren, *The Speaker's Sourcebook II* (New York: Prentice Hall Press, 1994).

Chapter 4

1. Having had a spiritual awakening as a result of these steps [i.e., the first eleven], we tried to carry this message to alcoholics, and to practice these principles in all our affairs.

2. Abraham J. Twerski, *The Spiritual Self: Reflections on Recovery and God* (Center City, MN: Hazelden, 2000).

Chapter 5

1. This section was adapted from Abraham J. Twerski, *The Sun Will Shine Again: Coping, Persevering, and Winning in Troubled Economic Times* (Brooklyn, NY: ArtScroll/Mesorah, 2009). Used with permission of the publisher.

2. René A. Spitz, "Hospitalism—an Inquiry into the Genesis of Psychiatric Conditions in Early Childhood," *The Psychoanalytic Study of the Child* 1 (1945): 53–74.

3. Rosalind C. Barnett, "Home-to-Work Spillover Revisited: A Study of Full-Time Employed Women in Dual-Earner Couples," *Journal of Marriage and the Family* 56, no. 3 (1994): 647–56.

4. Barbara Bailey Reinhold, *Toxic Work* (New York: Plume [Penguin Books], 1997).

Chapter 6

1. Abraham J. Twerski, *The Sun Will Shine Again: Coping, Persevering, and Winning in Troubled Economic Times* (Brooklyn, NY: ArtScroll/Mesorah, 2009). Story reprinted with permission of the publisher.

2. Abraham J. Twerski, *It's Not as Tough as You Think: How to Smooth Out Life's Bumps* (Brooklyn, NY: ArtScroll/Mesorah, 1999).

3. Glenn Van Ekeren, *The Speaker's Sourcebook II* (New York: Prentice Hall Press, 1994).

4. Abraham J. Twerski, *The Sun Will Shine Again: Coping, Persevering, and Winning in Troubled Economic Times* (Brooklyn, NY: ArtScroll/Mesorah, 2009). Story retold with permission of the publisher.

Chapter 7

1. Abraham J. Twerski, *Substance-Abusing High Achievers: Addiction as an Equal Opportunity Destroyer* (Lanham, MD: Aronson, 1998).

2. Rachel Naomi Remen, *My Grandfather's Blessings: Stories of Strength, Refuge, and Belonging,* paperback ed. (New York: Riverhead Books, 2001).

3. Elizabeth Arias, "United States Life Tables, 2004," *National Vital Statistics Reports* 56, no. 9 (Hyattsville, MD: National Center for Health Statistics, 2007).

4. Melonie Heron, Donna L. Hoyert, Sherry L. Murphy, Jiaquan Xu, Kenneth D. Kochanek, and Betzaida Tejada-Vera, "Deaths: Final Data for 2006," *National Vital Statistics Reports* 57, no. 14 (Hyattsville, MD: National Center for Health Statistics, 2009).

5. Cumberland Mountain Community Services Board, "Tranquilizers," http://www.cmcsb.com/tranquil.htm.

Chapter 9

1. Glenn Van Ekeren, *The Speaker's Sourcebook II* (New York: Prentice Hall Press, 1994), 106.

2. Brendan Gill, *Late Bloomers* (New York: Artisan, 1998).

3. Glenn Van Ekeren, *The Speaker's Sourcebook II* (New York: Prentice Hall Press, 1994), 61.

4. Ibid.

5. Ibid., 82.

6. Dov Moshe Lipman, *Time-out: Sports Stories As a Game Plan for Spiritual Success* (Devora Publishing, 2008).

About the Author

ABRAHAM J. TWERSKI, M.D., called by *Business Times* "Pittsburgh's most famous psychiatrist," served as a pulpit rabbi before attending Marquette University Medical School in Milwaukee and completing his psychiatric training at the University of Pittsburgh Medical School.

Dr. Twerski served as medical director of psychiatry at Pittsburgh's St. Francis Hospital, and in 1972, he founded the Gateway Rehabilitation Center for treatment of alcohol and drug addiction. He was the medical director of Gateway for thirty years and is currently medical director emeritus. He is the author of numerous books on addiction, self-esteem, and spirituality, including collaboration on four books with Charles Schulz, creator of the *Peanuts* cartoon strip. He has lectured worldwide—in London, Madrid, Johannesburg, Australia, and Israel.

Dr. Twerski is married to Dr. Gail Bessler-Twerski, a psychotherapist, and has four children. His first wife died of cancer after forty-three years of marriage.